MW00467331

FARM STRONG.

Faith, Family, Farm & Fitness

by
Charles Wooldridge Hatcher

Selah
Press
PUBLISHING

Farm Strong: Faith, Family, Farm, and Fitness
by Charles Wooldridge Hatcher

2nd edition
Managing Editor: Kayla Fioravanti
Editor: Anna Cooke
Cover Design: Daryl Stevens, Studio 202
Cover Image: Granddad Hatcher

Copyright © 2016 Charles W. Hatcher
ISBN-13: 978-0692816172 (Selah Press)
ISBN-10: 0692816178
Printed in the United States of America
Published by Selah Press

Disclaimer: This book tells the story of the Hatcher Dairy from the point of view of the author. Other people may well remember the events portrayed differently than they are presented here. Good faith efforts have been made to trace copyrights on materials included in this publication. If any copyrighted material has been included without permission and due acknowledgment, proper credit will be inserted in future printings after notice has been received. Although the author and publisher have made every effort to make sure all information is correct at press time, the author and publisher do not assume and hereby disclaim any liability to any party for any loss, damage, disruptions caused by stories with this book, whether such information is a result of errors or emission, accident, slander or other cause.

For information on getting permission for reprints and excerpts, contact: charleswhatcher@gmail.com

Author Website: Hatcherfamilydairy.com
Publisher Website: Selah-Press.com

The Right Place

Every day there's a wonder of a normal life
with every bale that I cut with a knife
For I am the new keeper of this land
I feel like my grandfather is holding my hand
This very place is hallowed ground
With my last name I can be picked from a crowd
Nearly 200 years of family and farm
A normal life could do me some harm

It can be quite mischievous from a stranger's eye
My ashes will be on this soil the day I die
Whenever there are troubles or doubt
I look up to the sky and know what I'm about
Just one glimpse of those pictures in time
I get the feeling of tradition and pride
What comes of this soil leaves a good taste
For that I know this is the right place

Charles Hatcher

Dedication

This book is dedicated to all past, present, and future farmers. May the Good Shepherd guide the future generations of farmers as they are challenged with feeding the world's ever growing population.

Psalm 23
The LORD *is* my shepherd; I shall not want.
He maketh me to lie down in green pastures:
He leadeth me beside the still waters.
He restoreth my soul:
He leadeth me in the paths of righteousness for his name's sake.
Yea, though I walk through the valley of the shadow of death,
I will fear no evil: for thou art with me;
Thy rod and thy staff they comfort me.
Thou preparest a table before me in the presence of mine enemies:
Thou anointest my head with oil; my cup runneth over.
Surely goodness and mercy shall follow me all the days of my life:
And I will dwell in the house of the LORD for ever.
KJV

CONTENTS

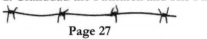
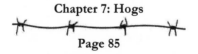

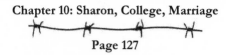
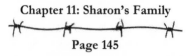
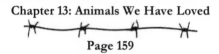
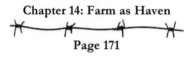

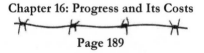
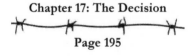

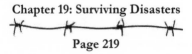

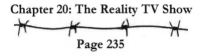
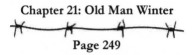
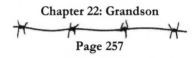
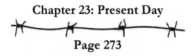

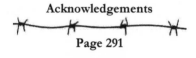
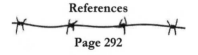

Prologue

I look back on my life and I wonder why. Why did everything happen the way it did? Why did the first Hatchers come to America in 1635? Why am I the way I am? Why do I live on a family farm? This book tells the story that answers these questions. It's a story of faith, family, friends, and a very special farm. We are all products of God's plan, our genetics, our environment, and the choices we make.

My journey through life is centered around the farm, starting with the childhood summers spent with my grandfather and extending to the present. This farm is still shaping me, molding me, filling my heart with love, and making me stronger every day. I want this story to move you, give you strength, and give you a full understanding of the importance of this farm—how the farm made me strong, and what *Farm Strong* means. I hope to describe the farm, people, places, events, colors, smells, and emotions in such detail that you feel it deep within your soul and become *Farm Strong* too.

This particular farm has been in the family since 1831. For six generations and nearly two centuries, family members have lived, worked, and died on this farm. My forefathers left this farm on occasion to go to war, protecting my freedom to live on the farm today. I walk on the same ground my father, grandfather, and great-grandfather walked on and took care of for so many years. I can feel their presence. To me this farm is more than a piece of dirt. It's God's creation, and it is just perfect.

Parts of this story are deeply personal, but I believe that

telling them is necessary for you to completely understand what's been important to me in my life. Perhaps there could be an application to your life. Let's begin!

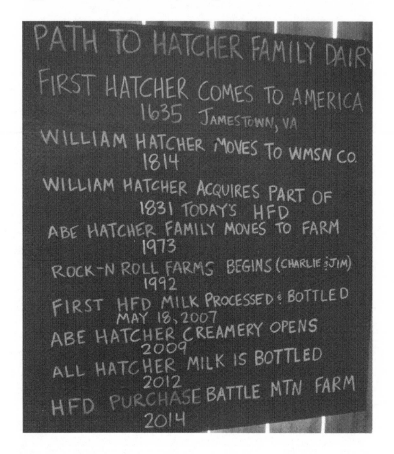

Chapter One

From the Beginning

In 1635, at the age of twenty-one, the first Hatcher stepped off the boat onto American soil at the settlement of Jamestown in the colony of Virginia in search of a better world. William Hatcher's arrival in America marked the beginning of the long journey which I am continuing today.

The ship records indicate that William made the arduous trip across the Atlantic Ocean from England to early America with no relatives accompanying him. Historical accounts are ambiguous as to whether William was married when he arrived and his wife joined him later, or if he selected a bride after arriving.

Either way, I can't imagine the courage it must have taken for William to cross the Atlantic with no family and begin a new life in a strange world. William adapted to his new environment rather quickly, settling in Henrico County, Virginia, to begin a life of farming and start a family. According to records, William had at least eight children. He acquired fifteen hundred acres of land, mainly from two land grants given in return for the transportation of six or more people from England to Virginia. Land grants to reward those who brought other people to the early colonies were customary at that time.

Tobacco was then the mainstay of the farming operation. William became a member of the early Virginia Assembly in the legislative body called the *House of Burgesses*, where he served at least two terms. Although well respected, he was known to have a fiery temper, and often displayed it in public when he shouldn't have. On one occasion, William called the Speaker of the *House of Burgesses* a "devil" during a heated discourse. His punishment was to apologize on his knees to the entire assembly.

I'm quite certain that the fiery temper trait, although somewhat diluted, has been successfully passed down through the Hatcher generations to the present. Hatchers remain the type to speak their minds even at the most inopportune moments. I'm lectured by my wife and children to keep my mouth shut on a regular basis, although I have never been jailed or had to give an apology on bended knee.

William was a rebel by any definition and apparently didn't want anyone telling him what to do, even the King of England. He participated in Bacon's Rebellion of 1676, which was a local uprising against the King's appointed governor in Virginia a full one hundred years before the Revolutionary War. William was old at the time of the rebellion, and though he did not actually fight in the rebellion, he participated by expressing his extreme displeasure with Governor William Berkeley verbally. The rebellion was squelched by King's troops arriving from England soon after it began. The only reason William didn't lose his head was that the King had mercy on William's "aged condition," fining him instead of taking his life. The fine was for eight thousand pounds of dressed pork for his Majesty's troops. To pay a fine of that magnitude, William must have been wealthy.

There was a tendency of the early Hatcher families to have ten to twelve or more children, taking the Bible literally when it said to populate the earth. One of William's sons was named Henry. In my direct lineage, the generations following Henry I were Henry II, Henry III, and Jeremiah, who was born in 1731. He was the first of many in a long line of prominent Hatcher Baptist preachers. Jeremiah and his wife Edith had eleven children, including my great-great-grandfather, William W. Hatcher. Jeremiah did not personally fight in the Revolutionary

War, although he did sign a document testifying to his allegiance to Virginia.

Apparently the Hatchers loved their new land, wanted independence from England, and didn't mind fighting for it. And fight they did! Every other available male Hatcher fought, including: William, Seth, Samuel, Obadiah, Josiah, John (Major), John (Lt.), Gideon, Fredrick, Daniel, Benjamin, and Thomas Hatcher. Some of the Hatchers lost limbs and some lost their lives. I'm proud to know that Hatchers were instrumental in American gaining her independence from England and the early formation of this great country.

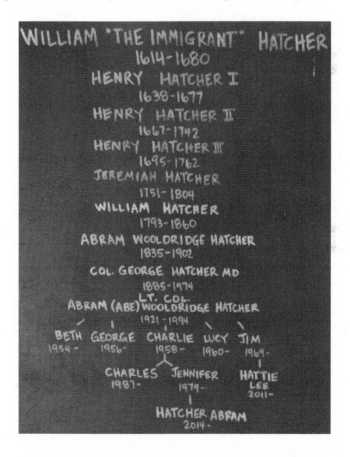

William W. Hatcher married Lucy Rucker in 1814 in Bedford County, Virginia. Soon after their marriage, the young couple moved from their roots in Virginia to Tennessee, settling in 1831 on part of the farm land we live on today. Wasting no time in starting a family, they produced twelve children, including my great-grandfather, Abram Wooldridge Hatcher. He was the eleventh child.

My great-grandmother Martha Elizabeth and great-grandfather, Abram Wooldridge Hatcher.

Abram married Mary Susan Dodson. At the time that the Civil War broke out in 1861, they had two young sons. The war had a profound effect on the farm and all those that lived on it. The Hatchers were not immune to the cruelty of war or the division that the war caused the nation, the states, and individual families.

Great-grandfather Abram Wooldridge Hatcher holding my grandfather, George Hatcher.

My great-grandfather, Abram Wooldridge Hatcher, and his brother, Spotswood Henry Hatcher, fought for the South, while their east Tennessee cousin John Hatcher fought for the North. Abram and Spotswood were both slaveholders. I struggle today with why Abram and Spotswood were slaveholders. How could they have owned human beings? During much of my boyhood years on the farm, I was raised by Lilly Mae, an African American nanny. Both Lilly Mae and my parents taught me not to be prejudiced against any color or type of person. I have to wonder about my ancestors' choices, but I don't really have an answer. I'm hoping someday maybe I can ask them.

No one describes the pain of war, the fate of our souls, or what is truly important better than Spotswood Henry Hatcher did in a letter dated July 8, 1864, to his wife from a camp near the Chattahoochee River. The things that matter become crystal clear in the heat of battle, looking death right in the eye.

My dear wife, I will be hurried and can't write much and the shells are flying and bursting around us continually. We have been under arms nearly all the time and most of the time in hearing of the balls and shells. Mary, there is no use trying to give you a description of what we have passed through since the 10th of May. Abe and I have both come out unhurt so far and I earnestly pray that God in much mercy may continue to spare us. We are both in excellent health and have been nearly all the time, nothing more than a cold or headache. Our company has been quite unlucky. We have lost four killed and Captain Wilson is mortally wounded. Bob Fleming has lost his leg. W. Price has lost his left arm. Of course we all dread being shot very much and there is some good men falling around us every day but nearly all think this will be the last year of the war. (God grant that it may.) I can tell you I would not pass through again what we have experienced in the last two months for all the wealth of the world. Yet there may be just as bad in store for us and doubtless many of us will yet fall victims to this cruel war. I want to live and die in peace at home with loved ones around. I want to be spared to try to lead my children to the rock that is higher than I. To instruct them and influence them to yield submissively to the will of God and obey his commandments. I think some-times that I am not really afraid of death but I very much dread death on the hands of men. I prefer falling into the hands of my maker, and I thank and praise his name that he has spared me thus far. And if we never meet on earth again, God grant that we may meet in that better land where all is joy and peace. Write every chance and continue to pray for us.

Your Husband,
Spotswood Henry Hatcher

I can't read this letter without getting choked up, knowing that Spotswood wanted so badly to get back to the farm to his wife and children. If he didn't, he would see them on the other side where all is peace and joy and love.

Spotswood Henry Hatcher surrendered to Union troops in Nashville, Tennessee, on January 10, 1865. He took the oath of allegiance to the United States on that day. The war was over for him. The war officially ended a few months later on April 9, 1865, when Lee surrendered to Grant at Appomattox Court House.

Abram Wooldridge Hatcher, my dad's namesake, was hit six times by battlefield debris—spent bullets and cannon balls—during the Civil War but miraculously was never seriously injured. He missed the bloody Battle of Franklin, which I believe was providential; otherwise, I feel sure he would have perished. The family story is that that my great-grandfather's commanding officer sent him home because he didn't think the Confederates would attack the fortified Union forces in Franklin.

The rumble of the Battle of Franklin could be clearly heard from the farm. As the crow flies, Franklin is a few miles away over Abe's Mountain. It's daunting to think that if Abram had been killed in the Civil War, the following six generations, including myself, never would have existed.

Hatchers taken in the 1960's.

The legacy of the Civil War has left visible marks on our farm in other ways, however: there are graves of slaves as well as slaveholders still on the farm property today that remind us of that dark period of American history. To better understand the connections between my family and the African Americans who lived on the farm as slaves, I turned to my good friend, the Reverend Jasper Hatcher, who is a Christian brother and an African American. Now eighty-seven years old, he has researched a lot about our families, and I received permission from him to include portions of his writings, which follow below:

"The Hatcher family of African American lineage from Williamson County, Tennessee, has roots that are deeply embedded within the College Grove and Arno communities. To understand a little more about this African American family and where their roots further lies [sic], we must take a glimpse at the white family of the same last name who settled in the area. The information gleaned from the history of the white Hatcher settlers of the area will be instrumental in helping members of the present of the present day African Americans trace their roots.

"The earliest known white settler with the name Hatcher to Williamson County, Tennessee, was slave-owner William Hatcher (1793-1866). William Hatcher migrated from Bedford County, Virginia in 1814 to Arno, near Franklin, Tennessee. His wife was Lucy Rucker who he married in Bedford, County Virginia.

The Hatcher couple had twelve children:
Octavius Claiborne Hatcher (1816-1856)
John Rucker Hatcher (1818-1857)
Margaret "Susan" Hatcher Early (1820-1889)
William H. Hatcher (1822-1843)
Bernard McKendree Hatcher (1824-1898)
Sarah Ann (Sally) Hatcher Andrews (1827-1879)
Thomas Logwood Hatcher (1828-1904)
Lucy Hatcher Gray (1830-1907)
Spotswood Henry Hatcher (1831-1891)
Edith Hatcher (1834-1835)

Abraham Wooldridge Hatcher (1835-1902)
Elizabeth Jane (Bet) Hatcher Pollard (1838-1919)

"The theory that relating a short history of early Hatcher slave owners from the College Grove, Locust Ridge area will aid African Americans of the same last name trace their roots, is an earnest attempt at a collective study. Perhaps this information can be of assistance to anyone who has interest in the matter.

"The white slave owner William Hatcher and his wife Lucy Rucker Hatcher of the Arno area owned three un-named slaves as early as 1820. His 1866 Will made provisions for ten of his children to receive one slave and $500 each. That early document paves an avenue for local African Americans of the last name Hatcher to investigate if one of their ancestors were among the slaves willed by William Hatcher to ten of his children mentioned below:

Son Octavius C. Hatcher–slave Peter
Son John R. Hatcher–slave Sam
Daughter Margaret Susan Early–slave Jane or Jinny
Son Bernard McKendree Hatcher–slave Davy
Daughter Sally Andrews–slave Peggy
Daughter Lucy Gray–slave Eliza
Son Abram Wooldridge Hatcher–slave Messer
Daughter Elizabeth Pollard–slave Pollina
Son Thomas Logwood Hatcher–slave Sam
Son Spotswood Henry Hatcher–slave Ben

"A few African Americans bearing the last name Hatcher from the Arno community may trace their roots through the slaves owned by William and Lucy R. Hatcher's son John Rucker Hatcher (1818-1857). At the time of John Rucker Hatcher's death, he owned fourteen slaves.

Ned–age 50 (Jasper Hatcher's great-grandfather)

Maria–age 40
Almeda–age 15
Nelly–age 17
Sam Jr.–age 12
Edmund–age 8
Winny Jr.–age 6
Meredith–age 4 (Jasper Hatcher's grandfather)
Isom–age 3
Sam Jr.–age 18
Dilsy–Age 30
Winny Sr.–age 8
Letty–age 6
Jane–age 16"
[End of excerpts of Jasper Hatcher's writings.]

Jasper's parents Marvin Sr. and Sadie Hatcher.

6 of Jasper's 8 children.

A week or so after my visit with Jasper Hatcher at his farm on Owen Hill Road in College Grove, Tennessee, one hot June afternoon, I drove a short distance to Locust Ridge Cemetery. It is located on a hill just off Arno College Grove Road. I almost immediately located the graves of Jasper Hatcher's grandfather, Meredith Hatcher (1858-1944), and his father, Marvin Hatcher (1895-1970), but could not find his great-grandfather's (Ned Hatcher's) grave. I knelt beside their graves on the grass in a moment of quiet and prayed. As I reflected there in the cemetery, I thought that I knew exactly what Dr. Martin Luther King was talking about when he said in his famous "I have a dream" speech that "I have a dream that one day the sons of former slaves and the sons of former slave owners will be able to sit down together at a table of brotherhood." Thank God that dream came true. The table was set and brotherhood was served. I look forward to one day in heaven sitting at that table with all the Hatchers who have gone before me, white and African American.

Jasper and me.

Trials and tribulations continued for Abram after the war when he returned home to the farm, his wife Mary, and his two young sons. In 1865, Mary died five days after giving birth to a third son. The infant lived about a month and then also died. Adding to the sorrow, the house burned to the ground around that same time. (A new house very similar to the old house was built near the creek and spring along Arno Road, where it remains today.)

Abram remarried on March 26, 1868, wedding Martha Elizabeth Chriesman. Martha was twenty-four and Abram was thirty-three. This union resulted in eight more children. The youngest child born was my grandfather, Colonel Dr. George Hatcher. George was born on June 21, 1885, when my great-grandmother was forty-one years old and my great-grandfather was fifty years old.

The Hatcher Homestead on Arno Road.

Abram died in 1902 when George was sixteen, forcing my grandfather to quit school to support his mother. All of George's brothers were already out of the house by that point. His oldest half-brother, James Chriesman Hatcher, M.D., died of typhoid fever while serving in the Spanish American War. This tragic event inspired George to eventually become a doctor.

Granddad was able to attend Battle Ground Academy (BGA) by working as the school janitor in exchange for tuition. He was asked to clean the gymnasium to see if he could fulfill the janitorial duties before the school management agreed to the deal. Times were so hard when George was going to school that George's mother often packed his lunch with breakfast remnants, which were biscuits spread with bacon grease. The bacon grease served two purposes: to soften the hard biscuits and add a little flavor, making the biscuits somewhat more palatable.

Granddad seated in the center of the photo.

The other boys affectionately called George "Grandpap" since he was so much older than they, and he was more of a father figure than a classmate. He excelled in sports and academics, eventually becoming senior class president, captain of the football team, and star center of the basketball team.

Granddad in the center of the front row.

Granddad graduated from BGA in 1910. After BGA, he was engaged for six years to the love of his life, my grandmother, Eula Lee. However, the couple didn't set a firm wedding date. During these years, Granddad enrolled at Vanderbilt University to become a doctor. In his second year of medical school, after he had taken a critical chemistry exam and felt fairly confident that he had passed, George picked up Eula Lee in a horse and buggy. He popped the question, "Will you marry me?" and she said "Yes."

They obtained the services of a local squire Justice of the Peace, Jake Levine, and were married that night in the streets of Nashville while seated in the horse and buggy. Although Granddad had given my grandmother an engagement ring, there was no wedding ring, since the impromptu wedding had left no time for shopping. The squire therefore left the wedding ring out of that part of the brief ceremony.

The newlywed couple took a train from Nashville to Franklin and then hired a horse and buggy to carry them to the farm about twelve miles away. When they arrived, George woke his mother from a deep sleep to tell her the good news. Of course she was tickled to death to hear the news, but she was a little rattled because she had made no preparations for the couple to spend the night.

George planned for his new bride to stay at the home place on the farm with his mother until he finished medical school. However, two months later, on July 20, 1912, George's mother (my great-grandmother) died of a massive heart attack while polishing silver near the spring just off the back porch of the house. Plans therefore needed to change regarding where Eula Lee could stay while George was in school in Nashville. Eula Lee moved back in with her parents until Granddad finished his junior year at Vanderbilt.

Granddad's Vanderbilt Medical School Graduation

That summer, Eula Lee and George camped out in an Army tent near the everlasting spring on the farm below, which is where my daughter Jennifer and husband are now living. *How cool is that?* I can't imagine of a more romantic way to spend a summer. Friends and relatives marveled at the young couple's living arrangements, thinking that it must be true love for them to camp out on the farm for that many months.

George graduated from Vanderbilt University the following year, 1914. In 1917, George joined the Army after the United States declared war on Germany. My grandmother finally got a wedding ring when Granddad went off to World War I. She felt that she needed to have a ring on her finger while he was away.

Granddad served as a medical doctor during WWI and was known as an excellent diagnostician. After WWI, in 1919, my grandfather's first job was at Central State Hospital in Nashville, where he practiced Psychiatric Medicine as assistant superintendent.

In the years that followed, Eula Lee gave birth to my dad, Abe, in 1921 and my Aunt Martha in 1924. Granddad took a position at Manhattan Hospital in New York City that offered the opportunity to become specialized in treating eyes, ears, nose, and throat. The specialty training took him to Austria for several months in 1927. During that time, the log cabin was built from old log corn cribs on the southern slope below the milk barn.

My Granddad and Grandmother during WWI.

This was to be George and Eula Lee's Tennessee home when they visited the farm and someday become a place where they could return and live in permanently. A New Jersey hospital hired Granddad as a department head where he could practice both Psychiatry and his newly acquired specialty as an ENT (ear, nose, and throat) doctor. The job came complete with a furnished home on the grounds of the hospital. Granddad happily practiced there until he retired in 1947 and returned to his beloved farm.

The only interruption was World War II. Granddad was called up for active duty in the summer of 1942 at the age of fifty-six. A three-hundred-and-fifty-bed MASH unit hospital, the 121st Station Hospital, was under his command in England, which was bombed several times during the war.

When a whole train load of injured soldiers came in from the European theater, they could be unloaded, transported, and triaged at his hospital within three hours. Granddad's hospital was one of the highest regarded military hospitals in England during the war. A memorial stands in Braintree, Essex, today in honor of the 121st Station Hospital and those that served there. A dedication ceremony for the memorial was held in 1992, fifty years after the first servicemen were treated there.

121st Station hospital in the European theatre during WWII.

Although Granddad retired to Tennessee in 1947 as a full colonel, he did not truly retire from the Army for a number of years. He served as the Veterans Administration Chief Medical Officer for the State of Tennessee, inspecting and managing veteran's hospitals until he was seventy-two years of age.

Granddad below the American flag on the left.

My father, Abe, also served during WWII. He volunteered to serve in the Army Medical Corp. Although he graduated from Harvard University in 1943, Dad was unable to attend graduation exercises because of deployment to the Pacific theater, first serving in the Philippines and later as a medic at the 13th General Hospital near Japan in Finaschafen, New Guinea. After the war, Dad was in the Army Reserves, serving in the Judge Advocate General's section most of his life until he retired in 1985 as a Lieutenant Colonel.

Dad expected to serve in the Korean War in 1953, but he was never deployed. I can remember Dad going to many army training exercises on weekends and weeks during the summer for years, as well as teaching evening classes in Nashville for the Army Reserves. I'm proud of my father and grandfather's service to this country. It amazes me that Granddad served in WWI and that he and Dad both served in WWII. My mother is receiving my dad's Army retirement benefits now, and we are grateful for them.

My dad graduated from Harvard in 1943.

My dad, Abe, around 1943.

Granddad, Colonel George Hatcher M.D., around 1974.

Chapter Two

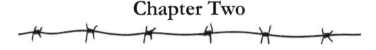

Granddad the Patriarch and His Farm

My granddad was George Patton-esque in behavior, style, determination, stubbornness, courage, and appearance. He had a fiery temper and a strong will, but also had a soft side and was very giving. By the time I knew him, he was bald and looked very distinguished. He was tall, measuring over six feet two inches, and this height has become a family trait: my dad and my brother Jim were also six foot two, and my cousin Mack Hatcher was nearly seven feet tall.

Granddad-full colonel.

Granddad was physically fit, strong, and handsome with sharp chiseled facial features, a prominent nose, and an especially strong jaw. You could open a bottle cap of *Coke* on the corner of his mandible. It's the same jaw that all Hatchers have to this day. The fiery temper has toned down through the Hatcher generations, but the family stubbornness still persists.

Granddad's farm attire was the same every day. He wore long-sleeved, light blue, all-cotton shirts. He buttoned the sleeves around his wrists and to the last button on the neck all the way up, just below the Adam's apple. I'm assuming he did this to protect his skin from the sun, insects, and barbed wire. He would complete the outfit with faded blue jeans that had a very high waistline.

I like to wear my jeans high as well; they just feel more comfortable that way. My kids are constantly telling me to pull them down. Granddad wasn't fat at all but had a prominent abdominal belly bulge below his brown belt. My dad had that same belly bulge, and I assume I will too if I live long enough. Granddad had no butt at all, just a back with a crack. This trait also has passed down to at least three generations so far.

Granddad's farm shoes were brown leather, ankle-high, lace-up boots worn with white socks. Granddad completed his farm attire with a mangled, brimmed, straw hat that was stained around the head band. He was outside in the sun so much that he had a tan line where the hat covered his bald head. Granddad tanned easily, so the skin exposed to the sun was bronze in color, while the top of his head remained lily white.

Whenever Granddad went out on the farm, he always carried a walking stick to assist his walking, sort livestock, and provide protection. He once used it to kill a rabid red fox that attacked him in the cedar tree thicket above the Robinson Hill barn. He then endured the series of forty plus rabies shots given in the stomach that were necessary at the time.

Granddad had a unique scent about him. It consisted of *Ivory* soap (which we all bathed in), *Tide* washing power, and *Old Spice* aftershave, all mixed with a hint of the same characteristic body odor my dad had. I'm wondering if I have the same body odor already, or if I'll acquire it as I get older.

Granddad was so hard of hearing that he couldn't even hear thunder. He wore a hearing aid in his left ear anytime he wanted to hear something. The hearing aid was connected to a shiny silver battery pack the size of a pack of cigarettes by a long white wire that dangled from his ear down the side of his head. The battery pack was tucked in the left chest pocket of that long-sleeved shirt. If you wanted Granddad to hear you speaking, you had to face him, talk slowly and loudly, enunciate well, and cast your voice directly at him. I suppose that's why Hatchers today talk so loudly—we all had to talk loudly as kids or we would never be heard.

During my granddad's lifetime, he amassed considerable wealth and property. He inherited only a small part of the farm from his mother when she died, but he grew it to nearly five hundred acres over the years. Granddad also purchased another five-hundred-acre farm on the southwestern end of the county.

He was a living testament to what working hard and persevering can accomplish, at least in that time and place. I'm not sure it's still possible to achieve what Granddad did in today's world.

He was compassionate in his own way. We still hear stories to this day of how he provided free medical care for someone in need or helped a veteran gain access to treatment at the veteran's hospital.

Granddad and my grandmother Eula Lee had two children, my Aunt Martha and my Dad, Abe. As wedding presents, Granddad gave one farm to each child. My dad was given part of the farm we are on today when he married my mother, Jacqueline (Jacque) Price, in 1953. *What a wedding present!*

Dad purchased Robinson Hill and also some bordering property from Pal Covington, increasing the farm to well over five hundred acres. My Aunt Martha and my dad each had five children. Aunt Martha and her husband Paul Cargo's children were, from eldest to youngest, Bill, Rachel, Libby, Sally, and Paul. I am the middle child of Abe and Jacque Hatcher, with two older siblings, George and Beth, and two younger siblings, Lucy and Jim.

Granddad was a leader in sports, a leader in his profession, a leader in the military, a leader in the community, and, most importantly, a leader of his family. He brought the family together like no other; family to Granddad was not only blood kin but everyone in the community.

Granddad's word was his bond. If he told you he was going to do something, you might as well mark it down because if he was still breathing, it would be done. Granddad was a Hatcher and instilled in us a family code of living: he didn't believe that Hatchers were better than anyone else, but he didn't want us to disrespect all the previous Hatchers gone by.

Granddad wanted us to live by the code set by previous Hatchers. And that's the way it was.

Granddad's farm: the everlasting spring

Water is essential to all life. That's the reason why early settlers and communities built near water sources, and my granddad knew its importance as well.

The farm consists of a series of beautiful rolling hills and valleys with some very fertile ridge tops that are fairly flat or are at least navigable with a tractor. Some of the hillsides can be mowed by a tractor, while some are just too steep to attempt to mow. We have some bedrock limestone in the valleys and some occasional sandstone in the hilltop fields. The topsoil on the hilltops is deep and rich and silty.

There is a twenty-five-acre field on top of one of those ridges. The field slopes off sharply on its north and south edges into hardwood trees and protruding ledges of rock. There are two springs on the north side and two springs on the south side of the field, where fresh water, clear and, cool, flows out between the shelves of rock. I have often thought there must be a large underground lake below the field supplying the springs. Only one of the springs has proven to be everlasting. It was important to have this, as Granddad knew he needed to secure a dependable water source for both man and animal. To reach the spring, one must to climb a fence and follow a path down a steep and treacherous slope to the spring about a hundred feet below. One false move on the way down to the spring could prove deadly. The path down from the spring is surrounded by oak, cherry, and ash trees majestically reaching towards the sky. Many of the trees are too large at the base for a person to reach around and touch his fingertips together. They are very old and have witnessed many historical events over the last two hundred years. The tree leaves form a solid canopy of protection from the elements. I was caught down near the spring one time during a severe thunderstorm and not only felt safe but did not get wet.

Granddad took extraordinary efforts to capture the spring water from this source and deliver it to many parts of the farm, ultimately constructing a simple but effective system. His plan was to have the spring water flow through galvanized pipes from the mouth of the spring to a sediment tank and then to a reservoir, utilizing the flow of gravity. The spring water was then pumped to another reservoir on top of the hill. Finally, the water was released from the reservoir to flow downhill and be delivered to a series of concrete water troughs for livestock.

Today we use this same system, except that we now have a submersible pump in the first reservoir, the second reservoir has been removed, and we have installed pipe all the way down to the bottom of the hill, nearly a mile away. Now this everlasting spring supplies three water troughs, my daughter's house on the top of the hill, and my house at the bottom of the hill. It could supply more. The spring is constant, clean, and pure, reminding me of all that is good in the world. The spring also has a spiritual connotation for me: the realization that God is everlasting, too, and will not abandon me, just as he continually provided for the generations who came before me through this spring of satisfying water.

Granddad's farm: the cabin

Granddad built a small log cabin on a two-acre lot below the milk barn, which is at on the southeast corner of the farm, in the late 1920's. The log cabin was assembled with the wood from two log corn cribs and an old cabin from Kentucky. The entire structure, except the shingles on the roof, was made of wood, including the floors, walls, and cabinets. The log cabin had five rooms on the first level: the kitchen, a dining room, a very small hall bedroom, a master bedroom, a half bathroom, and a full bathroom off the side entrance. There was also a second level accessed by a steep set of wooden steps to a bedroom and an attic.

The water source for the cabin and the milk barn was a well in the cabin yard. The cabin had no air conditioning. It was my home during the summers I spent with Granddad during the 1960's.

Granddad entertaining on the farm

Granddad was the original party animal. He loved to have parties in the cabin yard. Through these parties, he brought family and friends together and shared the love. These yard parties were the ultimate in social events in Arno, Tennessee, back in his day.

Preparation for these parties would begin days before the event. Granddad had a grill, constructed on the west side of the cabin yard, which was made out of rock collected off the farm. I can remember him gathering tomatoes, cucumbers, watermelons, and field corn. He liked onions and would sit in a chair skinning them himself. I tried to help Granddad with the onions once, but the onions were so intense that my eyes watered too badly to continue. He would dice the onions up, mix them with hamburger meat, and cook the hamburgers on the rock grill. If we didn't have hamburgers, we would have barbequed goat. The goat meat tasted a little gamey, but the smoked flavor and barbeque sauce made it quite tasty.

The field corn would be steamed, dressed with butter, or cut off the cob, making a sweet creamed corn. A watermelon was kept in the spring to chill a day or two before. The cut pieces of watermelon were intensely red with dark black seeds in the pulp. You had to lean forward when you took a big bite of the watermelon, or the succulent juice would run down and cover your chin and chest.

Granddad would make sweet southern-style ice tea with pure cane sugar and served it in a big tan crock. He had a large ladle to dip out the ice tea into glasses. Mint leaves from the plants that grew near the wet area around the well house were sprinkled into the crock, giving the tea just the right measure of mintiness.

Dessert was always hand-churned ice cream made of the rich whole cream from Guernsey cows that were being milked at that time. My favorite flavors were *Oreo* cookie and peppermint. Granddad would crumble up a whole pack of *Oreo* cookies or a whole can of the big sticks of the *King Leo* peppermint into the ice cream mix.

Family and community picnics in the cabin yard.

All the kinfolk and friends would arrive at the appointed time and park their cars in the cabin yard. Everyone always dressed in their Sunday best, with the women in dresses and the men in suits, ties, and suspenders. Men and women alike wore hats. Some of the ladies' hats had flowers adorning them.

The meal would be laid out on hay wagons covered with

table cloths. Tables and chairs set up under the maple trees were mainly reserved for the adults. While the adults conversed with each other, the kids would play in the cabin yard with first, second, and third cousins. It was heaven on earth, with a feast fit for kings.

Granddad

Chapter Three

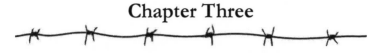

Grandkids at the Farm

During any given summer between 1960 and 1970, Granddad would host several grandkids plus some of their friends for parts of the summer on the farm. All of us would stay at the cabin. Granddad was in his late seventies and early eighties during that time. In the early 1950's, my grandmother, Eula Lee, had begun to suffer from "hardening of the arteries," which likely would now have been diagnosed as early Alzheimer's disease. For at least a decade, Granddad was the sole caretaker, only placing her in assisted living when her illness progressed beyond what he could manage.

By the early sixties, I remember Granddad bringing her out to the farm for occasional visits while we were there, but at that point communication with her was very limited. She died in January of 1968. I understand that she was an extraordinary woman and provided a counterbalance for Granddad's volatile temper and lack of patience. It was a shame I never had the privilege of knowing her before the onset of dementia.

Some of the best memories of my life are from those summers on the farm spent with Granddad, my siblings, and my cousins. Those memories are still vivid; if I close my eyes, I can see it all like it was yesterday. I'm going to do my best to tell you about some of those memories because that's when the farm first began to have a profound effect on me.

We grandkids weren't really scared of Granddad, but had a healthy respect for him. He commanded respect by his general demeanor; if he barked out an order, we followed it. He expected all of his grandkids to show respect to their elders. Any conversations we had with adults in those days always consisted of "Yes, sir" and "No, sir" or "Yes, ma'am" and "No, ma'am," or, after meal time, "May I be excused?"

My grandparents and parents, brother George on the left, sister Beth in the middle, I'm the baby and cousin Sally.

Granddad worked like a young man and did not tolerate laziness. He expected everyone to work as hard as he did. Granddad provided almost everything a kid could want: ponies, tractors, hay lofts, adventure, food, and shelter. If Granddad didn't provide it, the farm and Mother Nature did.

The farm exposed us to things that most kids might not ever see. Some things were good while others were bad. There was hard work, birth, death, disappointment, and joy. As I look back on it now, God really provided a training ground through Granddad and the farm in helping to shape us into what we are today. It was His plan from the beginning to make us stronger through our summer experiences on the farm with Granddad.

**The cabin in the early days,
note the old car to the left of the cabin.**

Breakfast, lunch, and dinner on the farm

Our days spent with Granddad during those summers were regimented. Everything was done at a specific time and a specific manner. We would wake up in the mornings at the same time, eat our meals at the same time, do our chores at the same time, and go to bed at the same time. I suppose Granddad had picked up that punctuality from being in the army for most of his life, and now he just preferred things to be that way.

Our days started at daybreak with the smell of coffee and the crowing of the roosters. Granddad would have been up for a while cooking our breakfast in a large and well-seasoned black iron skillet. We always had bacon or fresh sausage, pancakes with *Aunt Jemima* syrup—or hot biscuits or toasted *Sunbeam* white bread with *Smucker's* grape jelly and a generous portion of melted butter—and fresh eggs we had gathered the day before from the hayloft. Granddad preferred eggs sunny side up, so that's the way he fixed them for us. Every once in a while,

Granddad would cook country ham from the hog killing of the previous winter.

My personal breakfast favorite was the salty, red-eye, country ham gravy that Granddad concocted in the wrought-iron skillet out of black coffee and country ham remnants. There is nothing better in the world than a hot fluffy lard biscuit drenched with red-eye country ham gravy and choked down with a glass of cold, fresh milk. Breakfast was undoubtedly the biggest and best meal of the day. The breakfast bars I eat for breakfast today pale in comparison to these country breakfasts that Granddad lovingly prepared each and every day for his grandkids.

A distinctive brown-and-white, ceramic half-gallon pitcher was used every day to fetch fresh milk from the milk barn. After climbing up a short ladder on the side of the milk tank, we could raise the cooler lid and dip the creamy milk out. A glass of fresh, ice-cold milk straight from the cow is heaven in a glass. Large *Smucker's* jelly recycled glass containers served as our glassware. If the level of milk in the tank was too low for our short little arms to reach, Mr. Pagel was kind enough to dip the milk for us.

Mr. Pagel was the farm manager and primary milker of the cows. He lived with his family in the little white farm house above the dairy barn by the road. Mr. Pagel was short in stature, lean, and physically fit with bulging forearms like *Popeye*. He was bald and wore a faded green Army cap with his blue jeans—a lean thirty-inch waist. He smiled all the time, displaying beautiful pearly-white teeth. Mr. Pagel was a quiet man, very patient and amazingly tolerant of inquisitive children. He smoked cigarettes while he milked the cows. I always loved the smell of the cigarette smoke as it mixed with the green-grass aroma of the fresh cow manure and the sweet scent of the molasses-coated feed.

We would eat all of our meals around a large, square, oak

table with Granddad at the head facing us. He liked his coffee hot and would overfill his coffee cup so that it flowed into a saucer. He would then plant his elbows on the table, raise the saucer up to his mouth with both hands, and gently slurp the coffee, savoring with each sip.

I thought Granddad's best lunch-time dish was his baked chicken and rice. A whole chicken would be cut up into pieces while a batch of white rice was brought to a boil. After placing the chicken and rice in a large dish, Granddad would add a couple cans of *Campbell's* mushroom soup, and then bake it all in the oven until the meat fell off the bones. You could feed a lot of hungry young'uns with this dish, especially if you added some vegetables from the garden like tomatoes, boiled corn, and fried okra.

**Granddad making hamburger patties mixed with onions.
Cousin Rachel, Cousin Paul, and myself looking on.**

Granddad had a dinner bell mounted on a post at the screen door entrance facing the dairy that he used to signal meal time and family emergencies. When Granddad rang the dinner bell, you could hear it from all over the farm as it echoed through the hills. We would come running from all directions, knowing Granddad was calling us—no cell phone required.

By the end of the day, Granddad was winding down and would remove his hearing aid to disconnect from his surroundings and get some much-needed rest. The summertime kids effectively exhausted him. Most evenings, Granddad could be found fast asleep, emitting loud, intermittent snores from the big red easy chair, with the evening news playing on the small black-and-white television in the corner of the room. At this point, all we kids knew we had at least an hour of unsupervised maximum fun time.

We were left to fend for ourselves for evening meals in reckless abandonment. Our typical fare was *SpaghettiOs* out of the can, peanut butter and jelly sandwiches, or grilled-cheese sandwiches made with *Sunbeam* white bread, big hunks of *Velveeta* cheese, and voluminous amounts of butter. I loved to dip the corners of the gooey grilled-cheese sandwich into

Campbell's tomato soup, making sure the bread was saturated before consuming it.

After dinner, the kitchen was always a wreck, with tomato sauce, jelly, peanut butter, and unidentified smears on the stove, cabinet drawers, floor, and ceiling. Clean-up was accomplished by teamwork and an assembly line of cousins perched atop chairs against the kitchen sink to wash, dry, and store the silverware and dishes. All evidence of our unsupervised cooking fiasco would eventually be removed. Granddad would wake up from his evening nap just in time to put us to bed. I don't ever remember going to bed hungry. Our dinners at the farm taught me at an early age how to cook for myself and also how to always find something to eat in the kitchen—what I found to eat might not be my preference, but it would do.

Bedtime at the cabin

The sleeping arrangements depended on the number of grandkids and other kids that might be visiting the farm during the summer. If there were only a few grandkids, we would sleep in the small bedroom down the hall from Granddad's bedroom. If there were more than four or five kids, we would need to split up, requiring some unfortunate souls to sleep upstairs.

There was no air-conditioning in those days, and the hot, humid Tennessee summers could be downright miserable. For the unlucky few that slept in the upstairs bedroom, the relentless heat was stifling. There was only an attic fan to keep the oven-like air moving. I can remember lying there and sweating, moist and sticky, on the really hot nights, trying to go to sleep by counting sheep.

It was a nightly ritual for Granddad to tuck in every grandchild at bedtime, making sure we were each snug in our beds. It always went the same way. Granddad would tickle our bellies while he recited, "Good night, wake up bright, in the morning light, to do what's right, with all your might, good night!" The tickling intensified as he recited until we were giggling uncontrollably and hysterically into the night. After that, we would always say our prayers, most of the time out loud so that all could hear.

Games and playtime at the farm

Before the days of laptops, smart cell phones, social media, and digital games, we had great fun on the farm. The entire farm was our playground, and what a playground it was! On the farm, it was so easy to entertain ourselves with the animals, farm work, and all that Mother Nature had to offer.

One of the many places we played was along the cow paths coming down off the hill. Cows are creatures of habit. When the cows came to and fro from the pasture lots on the hill to be milked, each cow would follow the cow in front of her, single file, forming narrow, silty paths. After years of constant use, the paths formed deep earthen troughs like the track on an Olympic snow mobile course. In places, we kids could stand within the cow paths and the sloped sides would be well over our heads. This erosion has since been repaired and prevented by conservation practices, but in the 1960's, the hollowed-out cow paths were a wonderful place to play. We would run up and down the paths, play hide-and-go-seek, and attempt to scale the steep sides of the paths, falling and doing backwards somersaults for hours. We played in the dirt and dried cow manure like it was our own personal huge sand box, generously provided for us by the cows.

We had to share our play area with beetle-like insect creatures I called doo-doo beetles. This was their work area, and they were serious about it. They rolled particles of the dried cow manure in the dry sandstone dirt to make perfectly round doo-doo balls, just like they were making a snow man. We would play with the doo-doo balls like marbles. The balls were many times the beetles' body size. From their perspective, the balls were massive boulders. The strength of superman was required for the beetles to roll the balls. Their work was masterful, downright amazing, and nothing short of perfection.

We watched the beetles work for hours. For that length of time, we were in their fascinating little world and not ours: a microcosm of work and a display of what working together, doo-doo beetle style, can do. The focus the beetles had toward their task at hand is a good example for all of us. It reminded me of the construction of the pyramids by the Egyptian slaves. I think that the beetles had the same feeling of satisfaction after rolling doo-doo balls all day as we did when the last hay bale was placed in the barn. There is something about physical work and getting the job done, even if it's dirty, that is good. All creatures can experience it, even doo-doo beetles.

In this same play area, we made war—or rather, we played the ultimate war game. By today's standards I look back on this and realize it was dangerous, but boy, was it fun. Many of the things we did as kids in those days are not done today. I really see no reason how we escaped being blinded, deafened, or severely maimed.

Supplies needed for our war game were fire crackers, wet cow manure pies, and numerous cousins. All were plentiful. The object of this game was to cover the enemy cousin with as much wet cow manure, blasted by firecrackers from manure piles, as possible. We strategically placed our firecrackers in the wet cow patties, just like putting candles on a cake, and the cousin who set up the most fire crackers usually won, since this created a perfect minefield. As the enemy cousin would come down the cow path, the wet cow pies were spaced every few feet (because cows poop a lot). As the fire crackers went off, blasts of wet, green, delightfully smelly cow manure blasts would then cover the intended victim from head to toe. Larger blasts of cow manure could be created if numerous fire crackers were placed in the same cow pie, thereby increasing the intensity of the explosion. The end result of the war game was that all of us were covered with wet green cow manure.

If you were fortunate, you wouldn't have any cow manure in your mouth or on your teeth, but it was always in your hair and caked on your face. We could have passed for Navy seals, camouflaged and ready for covert operations. The declared winner was the one that had the least cow manure on them.

Clean-up was no problem. We would just take a dip in the farm pond on the way back to the cabin. The cows took dips in the pond, too. They looked like African water buffalo with only their heads and the tops of their backs exposed above water, cooling off and pooping and peeing in the pond at will. Most of the cow manure was removed from our clothing and bodies after the pond bath, but we reeked of pond algae, cow manure, and urine. We got a healthy dose of all manner of bacteria, a natural vaccination program with live organisms. Our immune systems were in over-drive but running smoothly. We never got sick.

Before entering the cabin, we took turns hosing each other off with the water hose next to the well house to rinse off the larger particles of pond mud and manure. Off the side back entrance and porch of the cabin was one of the two cabin bathrooms. This bathroom was designed to clean up filthy kids with a concrete floor and an open air shower—no shower stall or curtain—on the back wall over a floor drain. We used the same *Ivory* bar soap for cleanup that Granddad used on our bodies and hair. Shampoo was not usually available.

Our showering process was segregated, with the boys and girls taking separate group showers and going in turns to lather and rinse off under the shower head. The faint smell of cow manure and fishy pond mud was usually still present even after repeated *Ivory* soap applications and rinses.

Another favorite play area of ours was on the property line along the southernmost border of the farm. This was a favorite because of the massive oak trees, a farm pond, and the intense solitude. The only noises were those made by us, the squirrels scurrying along the tree branches, deer prancing, or acorns falling from the trees. Many kids (and adults, too) had carved their initials in the trees in previous years. I wondered whether any Indians, early settlers, or Civil War soldiers had done the same. All of us in those days carried a pocket knife to cut hay twine, castrate calves/lambs, or whittle arrows. The pocket knives were sharp, too. There was always an old man sitting on a bench in front of Arno store willing to spit sharpen our knives on a sharpening stone. I would just reach in my pocket and begin carving effortlessly my initials in the tree. I didn't think about it then, but I do now. I'm only on this earth for a short while, and I might as well leave my mark on our land.

One of my favorite activities during those summers with Granddad was going down to Arno Store. Arno Store was the old country store owned by Milton and Virginia Ryan less than a mile south on Arno Road at the intersection of Arno Road and Arno College Grove Road. Arno Store was the closest store to get essential farm supplies, the *Ivory* soap we used to clean off the cow manure as well as lunch without driving 15 miles to downtown Franklin, Tennessee.

Standard lunch fare for me was a bologna and cheese sandwich, potato chips, a *Moon Pie* and a *Sun Drop* in a glass bottle. The sandwich contained a slab of bologna and American cheese, a fresh cut tomato slice and a generous spread of mayonnaise between two slices of *Bunny* bread so large I could barely grip it with two hands. The items I had for lunch were all locally sourced long before the local food movement became popular. The store was run by Mrs. Ryan, a gun-toting, tobacco chewing, no nonsense operator. She often disciplined kids that came in the store with a swift kick or scolding in a day and time when most parents didn't mind others disciplining their kids.

Arno store burned down in the early 1980's never to be built back. For the most part, country stores have disappeared from today's rural communities, replaced with big-box stores. I miss the old-time country general stores. They provided friendly, necessary service for rural communities.

Work and a fall

We grandkids would often help unload the hay from the wagon by rolling the bales to Mr. Pagel or to Mr. Tomlin to place on the hay elevator. We weren't quite strong enough to pick the bales up, so rolling them was the best we could do.

For this hot work, we would drink water and *Kool-Aid* by the gallons. My favorite flavors of *Kool-Aid* were grape or strawberry. I can remember mixing the *Kool-Aid* powder with two quarts of the cold well water and adding a couple of cups of pure cane sugar. The well water tasted good, with a hint of limestone to it. There was none of the chlorine smell or taste that is typical with city water today.

On one particular day, my sister Lucy and Mr. Pagel's daughter were up on the load of carefully stacked alfalfa hay, about five levels high. I'm guessing the height from the ground was about fourteen feet or more. The girls were high atop of the hay wagon, alternately helping to unload the hay and playing, when, for whatever reason, Lucy lost her footing and took a swan dive off the top of that load of hay like a skydiver in freefall. She hit the ground face first with terrific force. Stunned and briefly knocked unconscious, Lucy lay still on the ground. From our view from the hay loft, we thought she was dead. For a few anxious seconds that seemed like an eternity, we waited to see signs of life. Miraculously, after a moment, Lucy gathered her senses, pushed herself up off the ground with her arms, and then slowly mustered herself to a standing position. Frothy blood streamed from her nostrils and she began to cry.

From a distance, something didn't look right about Lucy's face. I had to look at her twice before I realized why she appeared so odd. Her nose was to the side of her face. The sheer blunt trauma of the force of the fall had broken her nose, grossly altering her appearance.

Blood mixed with tears was rolling down her cheeks. At this point, Lucy began walking and then running toward the cabin, past the milk barn, and through the yard, crying and shrieking as she went toward the only person that she knew could help— her Granddad. As she neared the back porch door, Granddad emerged from the cabin side porch door as if on predetermined cue. He hesitated a moment to assess the damage, then calmly used his left hand to support the back of Lucy's head while firmly grasping her misplaced nose with his right hand. In one deliberate motion, before Lucy had time to think about it, he replaced her nose back to the center of her face.

Watching what had just happened confirmed to all of us what we had already suspected: Granddad was a good doctor and could fix almost anything. After all, he was a head, eye, ear, and nose specialist.

That night at the dinner table, total silence permeated the room. Granddad was visibly upset. We thought we were all in trouble for Lucy's accident and were bracing ourselves for the repercussions. Although he thought we shouldn't have been so careless, the main reason he was upset was because the accident happened under his watch. Throughout his whole life, he felt responsible for those under his command, and this was no different, since he was responsible for us, too. All of us breathed a sigh of relief because Granddad did not blame us.

The next day, Lucy's face was bruised and swollen to such an extent that it appeared that her face was flat. I really believe she had a concussion, not to mention blood clots, but she had one of the best doctors in the country watching over her. Over the next several days and weeks, the bruising on Lucy's face went through many of the colors of the rainbow—red, purple, green, black, blue, and all colors in between.

By the end of the summer, Lucy's nose and face had healed like nothing had ever happened. No ill effects! In fact, she went on to be a model starting at the age of thirteen and to make a living with her face. Lucy continues to be a model to this day.

Cousins at play in the cabin yard.
Note the rock grill at the back of the photo.

**Granddad scooping homemade ice cream
with me looking on.**

Chapter Four

Granddad's Livestock

Ponies and horses were a large part of those summers spent with Granddad. We had fun with them but also used them to do a little farm work, mainly sorting cattle and looking for any that were lost. The ponies were kept in the pony lot, which happened to be the same lot that housed the everlasting spring on top of the hill.

Cousins on a play ride across the farm.

Granddad gathered what he judged to be the gentlest of the ponies and kept them down close to the cabin for easy access during the summer months when the grandkids were around. The ponies were a permanent fixture of the cabin yard all summer. First thing in the morning, we would each catch ourselves a pony and bring it into the cabin yard. We were the original natural horsemen. Like the early American Indians, we used very little to control the ponies, just that rare direct connection between a person and an animal based on trust. A bridle, a rope halter, or grass twine strings were our only devices for guiding the ponies, when we used anything at all. It's amazing how timely leg pressure against a pony's sides can send signals as to what you want the pony to do. We hardly ever used saddles or saddle pads.

My dad on horseback.

I was the allergic kid in the bunch and was actually extremely allergic to horse and pony dander, but I did not let my allergies deter my pony riding activities. If I rode bareback, the inside of my legs responded with a terrible, itchy rash, especially if both the pony and I sweated. I could decrease my leg rash by riding on a burlap feed sack, but it sure didn't help much. In hindsight, the burlap feed sack probably wasn't the best material to use because of its abrasive nature, but sacks were plentiful and readily available. Application of cool well water to the rash or a dip in the shaded areas of the creek provided some relief for my discomfort.

Of course, all the ponies had names. The names that come to mind most readily are Sundance, Sunburst, Trixie, Cyclone, Jenny, Santana, Thunder, Lightning, Mayday, and HC, which stood for Hatcher Cargo. Most all of them were the pinto color pattern, either brown and white, black and white, or spotted— all of them except HC.

Left to right- Beth, Lucy, George and myself.

HC was a sorrel Tennessee Walking Horse with a big heart, and he stood about fifteen hands. He was as good a cutting horse—a horse used to sort cattle—as I've ever seen. He was trained by Vernon Pagel's son, Vernon, Jr. If you were actively "cutting" (sorting) or driving cattle, though, it was a real challenge to stay mounted, especially since we didn't ride with a saddle to hold onto. HC changed directions so quickly on his own that I found myself on the ground a few times. It just goes to show that you don't have to be a quarter horse, bred especially for sorting cattle, to be a good cutting horse; the Tennessee Walking Horse is a very versatile breed.

All of us were quite small in those days, so we developed a pretty ingenious method to mount a pony or horse that was too tall for us to just hop onto. After all, we didn't have the stirrup of the saddle to help us mount. As the tall horses or ponies we intended to ride grazed the lush cabin yard lawn with their heads down, we would straddle their heads. Once straddled, the pony instinctively raised its head and neck, effectively doing the mounting for us. The only problem was that we were facing the tail of the pony. Then all we had to do was turn around, and we were ready to ride.

The ponies and HC soon became wise to this technique and did their best to make it harder for us to mount with each attempt. We were not easily discouraged, though, and were usually successful after multiple attempts. Sometimes, if we didn't straddle the horse's head cleanly, we would be catapulted ten feet in the air, landing on the ground in the cabin yard with a thump instead of on the horse's back. This was by far more fun than any carnival ride you could devise. How we never got our necks broken, I'll never know.

These horses and ponies were smart. They really preferred lounging and grazing in the cabin yard to venturing out with a rider over the five-hundred-acre farm. Going out on the farm to them meant physical exertion and sweating, and they didn't want any part of it without a fight.

Our biggest challenge was successfully making it on horseback to the top of the hill. Once you made it up there, the reluctant pony or horse you were riding was convinced that you were serious about taking the ride and relented. Many times, one might need three attempts with a lot of persuasion to successfully make it to the top of the hill.

The ponies that were smarter (or more stubborn, depending on how you look at it) would bolt or run back to the cabin yard at break neck speed. I guess that's what they considered the home stretch. The closer to home the pony got, the faster it would run. The dash back to the cabin yard would be by far the most the chosen fine steed had exerted itself all day.

Salting the cows

Granddad had a baby-blue, four-door *Mercury Montego* sedan that had three speeds on the column and bad shocks. He used it as a farm truck and kept it in the old wood shed garage near the log cabin. Although Granddad would use the *Montego* for checking on all the farming activities, its primary use was for salting and counting the cattle. Cattle must consume salt on a regular basis for many physiological functions. If they don't get it, they will crave it and sometimes lick or eat dirt in an attempt to obtain the necessary sodium chloride. Plain white salt was Granddad's salt of choice. It was kept in an old, galvanized two or three-gallon pail in the trunk of the car, and he refilled the pail from bags of salt kept in the garage.

We would all pile in the old *Montego*, and kids would fill the front and back seats before Granddad headed out on a cattle salting adventure. First stop was the terrace lot, which was the first lot on top of the hill on the south side. It was an eighteen or twenty-acre field, with terraces three or four feet in height and ten to twelve feet in width that ran north to south across the steeper slopes of the field. They ran diagonally to prevent soil erosion.

Opening the gates to gain access to the fields was usually the responsibility of the youngest or the most willing passenger. This was often the time when a scuffle would break out amongst the kids in the back seat of the *Montego* as we fought to determine who would open the gate. The loser opened the gate. Opening gates is a way of life on a farm with livestock, but is totally foreign to urban dwellers.

Upon entering the terrace lot, Granddad would begin to

rapidly accelerate in order to gain enough speed to have any chance at all of crossing the formidable terraces. If the *Montego* didn't cross the terraces at an angle with a considerable rate of speed, it would bottom out on the frame against the terrace and get stuck. If that occurred, someone had to bring one of the farm tractors to dislodge the *Montego*, virtually bringing our salting adventure to a halt.

Ordinarily, though, we would cross those terraces in the old *Montego* like a Viking ship in high seas, sailing up and down over the waves and tossing about freely all passengers within. Our butts would be lifted off the seats, suspended in animation, with our heads hitting the car roof on each successive terrace crossing.

Upon reaching the salting location of his choice, Granddad would get out of the *Montego*, cup both hands around his mouth, and start calling the cows. He would holler "suuuk cow" or "whoo" at the top of his lungs, and his cow call would echo distantly down through the valley for miles. The cows would come running like they had been summoned to an important event by God himself. Granddad would then take the galvanized bucket out of the trunk of the car and proceed to walk around, periodically pitching handfuls of salt on the ground.

You could hear the cows ravenously licking the piles of salt, with their long rough tongues making sounds like sand paper on a rough wood surface. The cows always appeared grateful, occasionally looking up at Granddad intently for an instant and tilting their heads sideways as if to say thank you. The whole process was very satisfying for us and the cows alike.

Another reason for salting the cows was to create an opportunity to count them. If one were missing in a particular lot, a search party would be sent out to locate the missing cow or calf. Granddad always made every effort to find the missing and the lost—these animals were important to him. Counting, feeding, and caring for the animals on our farm were just some of the responsibilities Granddad taught me during those summers I spent with him.

Goats

Goats will eat almost anything. They will eat weeds, mature grasses, and other plants that cows and other animals find distasteful. Hence, Granddad kept the goats in the pasture lots that were full of rocks or of brush, or that were just hilly. A tractor and mower could not be used in these lots where unwanted weeds, mature grasses, and overgrowth were abundant.

Goats will graze and browse. They eat weeds, grasses, and leaves regardless of how high or low the plants are relative to the ground. Often goats will stand on stumps, rocks, fallen trees, or whatever is available to reach leaves or thistle blooms. The end result of the goats' eating habits is a pristine, well-groomed pasture lot that even an army of grounds crew maintenance workers could not accomplish.

Granddad had both sheep and goats. They were not only used as weed and brush removers, but also for meat production. The yard parties Granddad hosted in the cabin yard for relatives and the community often featured barbequed goat. It was also traditional for many people to have barbequed goat during the July 4th holiday weekend.

On Friday morning of the July 4th holiday weekends, people in cars and pickup trucks would be lined up in the rocky pasture lot near Arno Road behind the stock barn before daylight to select their goat(s) to barbeque. We would have rounded up all the goats the evening before, containing them in the stock barn. Eager buyers would pick the goat(s) they wanted from the group in the barn.

My football tackling skills were developed early as a result of the goat roundup and rodeo. You had to be as quick as a Ninja, have cat-like reflexes, and possess the grip of a gladiator to capture and hold one of those nimble goats. It was like trying to tackle an antelope jumping through a flaming ring of fire at the speed of light. The goat you had chosen to catch would launch itself up in the air just as you began to reach for it. I would catch a glimpse of tiny hooves flashing by the side of my head during the escape flight. It was all great fun until I actually caught the goat and it began to cry like a baby in distress.

The goats were mostly loaded into the front or back seat or the trunk of a car. Occasionally, a pickup truck, equipped with homemade wooden cattle racks that were rickety with age, would transport the goats. I often wondered whether the buyers would ever make it to their destination without the goats escaping. The realization that these goats would soon be sacrificed for the 4th of July celebration would begin to sink in around this point in the process. I remember that these occasions prompted me to realize for the first time as a child that some animals are used for food, and that that is their purpose.

One year, several weeks before the goat round-up, dogs got into the goats. We arrived with Granddad to witness a horrific scene of death, dying, and destruction. The bleating of goats, like the moaning of injured soldiers on the battlefield, could be heard coming from across the field. Torn raw flesh was visible hanging from the rear legs, necks, and ears of the downed dead and dying goats, with crimson red blood glistening on their lily-white, hairy coats. About six or seven dead and injured goats were scattered across the field. I became sick to my stomach.

Granddad pulled out a high-powered rifle from the seat of the *Montego*. He carefully and deliberately took aim at a dog that was still ravaging one of the goats. A shot rang out, and the dog fell dead beside the mortally wounded goat. Two or three other dogs scattered and ran for their lives after they heard the gunshot.

We ran over to the lifeless dog and rolled it over. I was horrified when I realized it was the family dog, Tip.

At that moment, many questions ran through my mind. How could Tip do this to other helpless animals? How could Granddad kill Tip? Seeing the death and destruction both of the goats and Tip left me feeling empty. To Granddad, the goats were his responsibility: they had a purpose, and it didn't matter whose dogs did the killing. The penalty for them was still death. I had just learned another important lesson from Granddad: there are penalties for bad choices.

Chapter Five

Alfalfa Hay and Fescue Seed on Granddad's Farm

Alfalfa

Alfalfa hay is excellent forage for dairy cows, but it requires fertile, well-drained soil to thrive. That's why Granddad planted alfalfa hay in the big field above the everlasting spring on the hill. The deep brown, almost black, silty topsoil in the field was twenty to thirty feet deep. The field grew such good alfalfa that it reached knee height and matted to the ground. Mr. Pagel cut the alfalfa with the *Ford Dexter* blue-belly tractor with a three-point hitch, six-foot-swathe sickle mower. It was difficult to cut; two days were needed to cut the entire field. In the end, there was a sea of good alfalfa hay laid on the ground in row after row.

Granddad weighing a hay bale.

The alfalfa was so thick that it required at least two days of curing with good, sunny summer days. Brimmage Tomlin, an older gentleman who worked and lived on the farm, would always do the hay raking. His tractor of choice for raking was a grey-bellied *Old Major Diesel Ford* tractor. He raked the hay with intensity, hands tightly gripping the steering wheel and the upper body slumped slightly forward. He resembled nothing so much as a scarecrow, albeit a very focused one. Mr. Tomlin was steady and persistent all the way until the end of the job.

Mr. Pagel baled the hay with the newer but smaller *Ford Dexter* blue-belly tractor and the old *Massey Ferguson* square baler. This was before the days of the big round or roll balers, and it was a time when people would routinely complete a full day of hard physical labor. These days, it is difficult to find farm help that is willing to handle small square bales.

The bales dropped out of the back of the baler onto a slide one at a time until the field was peppered with hundreds of bales. For us kids, the sight of bale after bale peppered all over the landscape was a daunting one. The field ordinarily produced well over fifteen hundred bales of excellent quality alfalfa hay, each weighing fifty to seventy pounds. Someone had to load all that hay onto a wagon one bale at a time to take it down to the hay barn, which was at the bottom of the hill and adjacent to the milk barn.

Mr. Pagel and his son, Vernon, were the most proficient hay handlers on the farm, although they had very different physical attributes. Vernon Sr. was more compact, shorter, and heavily muscled, while Vernon Jr. was tall, lean, and looked more like a swimmer; both, however, were fantastic hay haulers. Their skill at both throwing and stacking hay amazed me. With great finesse they could sling a bale of hay and firmly land it exactly where they desired.

Only the most skilled hay stacker could make a wagon load of hay that could withstand the trip down the steep hill. The bales needed to be stacked and intertwined in such a way as to tightly secure the load of hay on the wagon. The slightest shift in the hay stack risked the whole load being dumped. Yet I don't ever remember a load of hay stacked by Vernon Sr. or Jr. that was lost.

Since none of us kids were very strong at that young age and couldn't load a heavy bale on to the wagon by ourselves, the role of driving the tractor that pulled the hay wagon out to the field usually fell to one of us. The remaining kids would double or triple team the bales, either rolling or carrying them in unison to the wagon. It was a real struggle for us to load the bales onto the wagon bed. Vernon Jr., on the other hand, could sling a bale of hay with those long, slender arms to the top of a hay stack five or six levels high. He was amazing.

Even harder work—or at least hotter work—awaited us at the bottom of the hill, where the hay needed to be unloaded and stored in the barn's hay loft. The old hay barn was equipped with a rail system to spear and move hay stacks into the hay loft, a method used before it became standard practice to bale hay. Baling as we do today compacts the hay, allowing a larger volume of hay to be stored in the barn. The old, rusty, rail system remains near the crest of the barn roof today as a reminder of how things were once done.

Even the rail system was an upgrade on previous storage methods, though. In the days prior to my childhood, the hay had to be loosely stacked in a pile on the back of a wagon. The wagon would carry the hay down the hill, where it would then be unloaded by piercing the hay stack with the hook, raising it up to the rail, rolling the hay stack to the back of the barn, and then releasing it. My great-grandfather had done the same thing we were doing, only in a slower and harder way. Nevertheless, he must have had the same feeling of accomplishment as we do today when the hay is finally safely stored under cover.

In the late 1960's and the early 1970's, we used two hay elevators to unload the hay. A first hay elevator carried the hay from the hay wagon outside the barn into the barn on a chain with a set of dull teeth on it. The teeth stuck into the hay bale deeply enough that the bales didn't slip off. The chain was powered by either an electric motor or the PTO (Power Take Off) of a tractor. The first elevator sat on a wagon out in front of the barn and was projected upward at a forty-five degree angle to the top of the barn. A second elevator, suspended from the barn roof or supported by a stack of hay, was attached to top end of the first elevator to carry the hay to the back of the hay barn.

One could hear the constant chain-rattling of the hay elevators as bale after bale made its way up the first elevator to the second elevator, dropping off at the back of the barn. If the crew on the wagon unloaded the hay quickly, the bales were almost end-to-end as they made their way up the elevators in a continuous convoy. The hay stacking crew in the barn had to work fast just to keep up.

Mr. Tomlin always warned us about getting too hot. He

called it "getting the white eye." He was referring to heat exhaustion, when a person pales around the eyes and then passes out. I never "white eyed" while hauling hay, but I was well accustomed to the hot conditions and drank a lot of water. I can see how someone not accustomed to the conditions could easily overheat.

In the hay loft, there would be an assembly line of people in a row, slinging bales from one person to the next and then finally back to the unfortunate stacker. I always thought it was better to be outside the barn unloading hay than in the barn stacking it. Even though you were in direct sunlight outside, at least there was some air movement. In the loft there was no air movement, and working up against the tin roof of the barn was like being in an oven, except worse, since you couldn't get away from it.

The last bale of hay

The big hay barn down at the bottom of the hill would hold nearly three thousand bales when completely full. By the end of the summer, it would become apparent to me that we would fill the barn up. By that time, load after load of alfalfa hay would have been loaded in the big field above the everlasting spring, brought down the steep driveway, and unloaded one bale at a time onto the elevators. The back of the barn was stacked first as the bales came up the first elevator, gently dropped off onto the second elevator, and then on to the person below. The incessant chattering of the elevators' chains as we worked was a constant reminder that our work was not done.

I always thought the hay stacking crew had the hardest job, especially the hay stacker at the back of the barn. The stacker handled every bale and had to stack it several levels high. It was his job to neatly stack the hay so as to fit as much hay as possible in the barn. There was no breeze stirring in the hay loft, the air was thick with hay dust, it was hotter than eight hells, and you had to dodge the abundant, dive-bombing red wasps that liked to attack you.

The broken alfalfa leaf pieces stuck to all the sweaty exposed skin surfaces on our bodies: around the neck, the arms, and sometimes the chest and waistline. The light reflected off the sweat, causing all the exposed skin to shine brilliantly. Between loads, we were careful to remain hydrated and to cool off by drinking the cool cabin well water, hosing off our alfalfa-leaf-covered arms, and splashing our faces with double handfuls of the refreshing water.

The back half-floor of the barn was lower than the front half-floor of the barn. That meant that we had to stack the back half-floor four levels high with hay to get even with the front half-floor of the barn. Once we reached that point, we could stack the entire barn evenly from back to front until we got so high that the second elevator had to either be removed from the loft or tied to the rusty rail atop the eve of the hay barn. Eventually, the hay would be stacked right up to the tin roof, first in the back of the barn and then filled in all the way to the front of the barn. Several thousand bales later, the last bales would be ceremoniously placed in the remaining slots. Then we would descend backwards down the hay elevator, triumphantly hoist the elevator down from the loft, and cheer in jubilation.

The satisfaction of a job well done was immense. The realization of what we had accomplished would all come tumbling in: the hard work, blisters, blood, sweat, and tears suddenly would seem worth it. We had done all this for the milk cows that we depended on for so much, ensuring that they would have something nutritious to eat during the winter months.

Fescue seed

In the terrace lot, on the south side along the top of the hill, fescue grass was abundant and well established. Fescue grass is an excellent grass to plant in hilly fields to protect them from soil erosion. If it were allowed to mature, the fescue grass seed would hang heavy atop the long, slender stems. The seed fetched a handsome price per pound, so Granddad would combine and sell it on the open market as another source of farm income. Combining was accomplished with an old, orange Allis Chalmers combine, pulled and powered by the blue-belly *Ford Dexter* tractor. The combine had a sickle cutting bar that cut the fescue low to the ground. Once cut, the entire fescue plant, seed still intact, was carried into the combine by a moving black canvas pick-up. There it would be thrashed by the internal workings of the combine. The finished combined fescue seed came down a four-by-four-inch tube to the sacking apparatus.

The sacking apparatus had two metal benches, one on each side of it, so that an attendant could sit on each bench to sac the fescue seed. The grandkids were the attendants. Large burlap sacks were used to attach to the split dual head of the sacking apparatus. As one burlap sack filled with fescue seed, a lever was switched, causing the seed to go down the other tube to the awaiting empty sack.

The full burlap sacks of seed were heavy, weighing around eighty to one hundred pounds. It was all we could do to drag the full sacks out from under the sacking apparatus. We would tie full sacks at the top after gathering the loose edges together with grass baling twine, then drag them over to the slide that was attached to the side of the combine, release them onto the slide, and watch them gently fall to the ground.

The burlap sacks were abrasive to our bare arms as we handled them, causing a wide-spread rash on the inside of our arms on any exposed skin. We soon learned to dress like Granddad, with the long-sleeved, all-cotton shirts that could protect our arms when we were combing fescue.

The sun would beat down on us all day. A cloud of dust always followed the combine as the fescue seed was thrashed. At the end of the day, the full burlap bags of seed would be carefully loaded onto the wooden flatbed of the old *Studebaker* two-ton truck. Mr. Pagel and his son Vernon Pagel could load the sacks by themselves. My brother George and I would team up, one of us on each end of the sack, and load the full sacks in a swinging motion on the count of three. When the *Studebaker* truck was full, we and Mr. Pagel would head to the granary in Columbia, Tennessee, to sell the seed.

A trip to the big city was one of the few times we had the opportunity to have soft drinks during the summers with Granddad. He always gave each of us enough change to purchase a *Sundrop*—a local lemon-lime soft drink—and a *Moon Pie*—a southern chocolate-marshmallow delicacy—for our road trip to Columbia. The *Sundrop* didn't always go down smoothly as we weren't accustomed to carbonated drinks. Often, the strong carbonation would cause the *Sundrop* to go down the wrong way, flushing our sinuses and blowing out our nostrils in a burning circuit. It was worth it, though; we only made the trip to Columbia once a year.

Chapter Six

Family Moves to the Farm

My father, Abe Hatcher was a patent attorney. These days, they call his specialty intellectual property law. Dad was very intelligent and had at least five college degrees: one in English from Harvard, degrees in chemistry, math, and agronomy from Tennessee universities, and a law degree from the University of Tennessee. He attended college for more than twelve years, making his studies a career.

Dad had already started medical school at Cornell University before he found his real passion. Granddad always wanted him to be a doctor. He lasted one semester before dropping out; Dad was book smart but had little every day practical sense. Dad couldn't hook a plow up to a mule or tractor, but he could work a calculus or physics problem, write a thesis, give a speech, interpret soil test results, win a debate, read music, and sing like a bird. Dad was the most giving person and the finest example of a Christian I have ever known. Ask anyone who knew him, and they will tell you the same thing.

My father and mother were ten years apart in age. When they married on June 20, 1953, Dad was thirty-one years old and Mom was twenty-one. Mom looked like a princess when they married. Hatchers are generally a fertile bunch, just like our ancestors. Mom and Dad proceeded to have five kids: Beth, George, Lucy, Jim, and me. I am the middle child. All of us were all two years apart in sequence except for our baby brother Jim, who came nine years after Lucy. We believe he was an accident.

Dad was very good at what he did and worked for several companies. During his years of practice in intellectual property law, Dad obtained many patents for his clients, some of them for high profile products like *Super Glue*. Most notable of the companies was *Eastman Kodak* and *Alcoa Aluminum*. As a result of his talents, Dad worked all over the Eastern United States, and the family lived in several states through the 1950's and 1960's as Dad changed companies or assignment locations.

The children were born in multiple states. My sister Beth was born in Miami, Florida. My brother George and I were born in Huntsville, Alabama. My sister Lucy was born in Rochester, New York, and my brother Jim was born in Pittsburgh, Pennsylvania. The family lived in three different places in and around Pittsburg, Pennsylvania.

In the winter of 1971, the course of our lives changed forever. We got word from Tennessee that Granddad had had a major debilitating stroke. We traveled to Tennessee as soon as we could after we heard the news. I had just started the seventh grade in middle school.

I can vividly remember arriving at the cabin to see Granddad. Granddad insisted on going out into the cabin yard. The stroke had paralyzed one side of his body, making it difficult for him to walk and talk. We assisted him outside into the yard. His speech was slurred as he began to talk. He was trying really hard to say something, but he couldn't get it out and we couldn't understand him.

All Granddads' life, he had been in charge, and now he wasn't. He was mad as hell because we couldn't understand him. The Hatcher fiery temper was about to explode. For some reason when he cussed, every word was clear and easily understood. When we got him to the large maple tree in the front yard, he began to cuss loudly; but it was plain as day as to what he said, "Sell the farm, sell the son of a bitch!"

He said it again while wildly slinging both arms in synchrony along his sides up over his head, "Sell the farm, sell the son of a bitch!" (I, my brother Jim, and my son Charles make this same slinging arm movement gesture today; apparently, we Hatchers can't appropriately communicate without using out hands and slinging our arms.)

I could see the pain of it all in Granddad's contorted face. I knew from his face that he didn't mean what he had just said. Granddad loved the farm. The last thing he really wanted to do was to sell it. He blurted that out about selling the farm because he wanted to protect my father from all the pain, work, and sacrifices that a farm can demand from its caretaker. Granddad had protected and sheltered his children all his life. He wanted nothing but the best for them, and that did not include the continuous hardships that a farm mandates. Granddad knew keeping the farm wouldn't be easy and could be a burden. *Boy was he right about that!* My resolve to keep the farm at all costs started then, at that moment, because I knew how important the farm really was to Granddad. He had worked his whole life to keep the farm going.

Over the following weeks, Granddad had a series of further debilitating strokes, necessitating his move into a nursing home. Granddad was okay with the nursing home. He actually wanted to go there, thinking it was easier for Dad, but I hated it for him. The smell and despair that I as a thirteen-year-old felt permeate the air in the nursing home is still vivid in my mind. I did not visit Granddad very much while he was in the nursing home. It wasn't that I didn't want to visit Granddad; I just didn't want to go to the nursing home.

In 1973, the Abe Hatcher family moved from Pennsylvania back to Tennessee in order to attend to the family farm and to take care of Granddad. His condition worsened, and a final stroke took Granddad's life in March of 1974. We lost a great man from what many view as one of the greatest American generations. I will forevermore remember Granddad as being larger than life and bulletproof, seeing him as a John Wayne or Ronald Reagan type who was mounted proudly on a horse against the panorama of the sky.

We moved into the Hatcher home place, the same farmstead house in which my great-grandfather and great-grandmother, Abram Wooldridge Hatcher and Martha Elizabeth Chriesman, lived a hundred years earlier in the curve of Arno Road on the eastern edge of the farm.

Although the original house burnt down just after the Civil War, the house as it stands today was built on the same spot. It's a two-story, white farm house made partially from logs and featuring a front and side porch. Arno Road was a dirt road until sometime in the 1950's when it was tarred and chipped. My sister Lucy and her daughter Jessica, along with Lucy's husband, Tommy, own and live in the Hatcher homeplace today.

There are at least three good water sources near the house: a small, babbling creek that runs through the middle of the farm, a little spring lined with sandstone rock and set about thirty feet back from the house, and a larger spring across the field behind the house. The larger spring was the main water source for the house. The water was provided by a spring house pump, pressure tank, and galvanized pipe buried in the ground across the field, much like the method used to transport water from the everlasting spring.

The transition from suburbia to country living was difficult. The days of riding bikes in the subdivision, tracer gun battles in the basement with friends, and having the responsibility of only having to take care of oneself were all over. Now we had the responsibility of taking care of the farm and everything on it.

Life on a farm is much different from city life. Between the livestock and the crops, coupled with the constant financial pressure, there is always something to do. Many of the chores are a real necessity. The animals' lives depended on us.

Livestock require the same things we do to survive—food, water, and shelter. The cows have to be milked and all the livestock tended to every day. Someone has to be on the farm, constantly working, three hundred and sixty-five days a year. I did not fully understand all of this at first, but did soon enough.

My experience during those summers on the farm with Granddad proved handy. *Could we effectively manage the farm without Granddad?* I wondered. Time would tell. Let the farm life begin!

The Hatcher home place, in the curve of Arno Road. Notice the dust on the roadsides.

I attended College Grove School from the seventh grade through the eleventh grade. The change from school in Pittsburgh, Pennsylvania, to College Grove, Tennessee, was dramatic. I guess the biggest shock was the move from a suburban area to a predominately agricultural community where farming was a way of life. However, even then one could already see a gradual decline in agriculture starting in the late seventies, though not near the accelerated decline that came in during 1980's and has lasted to the present day.

Everyone then knew where their food came from and understood the importance of agriculture, which is very unlike today. From the onset at school, the focus was on agriculture, too. The agricultural classes—called Future Farmers of America—were held in a little block building away from the main school building. Both boys and girls attended these classes. Part of the educational training was held in the school shop off the back of the block building. In the shop, we learned how to do things like welding, small engine repair, basic plumbing, and electrical wiring—practical things that one needs to know when farming and in life generally, but which few know today.

In Future Farmers of America class, we had training in all manner of topics ranging from soil science to plant science to and public speaking. All the members of the Future Farmers of America had dark blue, well-fitting jackets with pins which indicated accomplishments along the way. Some had more pins than others; my jacket still resides in my closet with a very few pins and is way too small for me to wear. In those days, it was common for boys and girls to have excused absences for farming activities such as hauling hay, straw, or tobacco. In fact, local farmers needing help for hauling hay or working in tobacco came by the school to recruit. The coaches of the basketball and football teams excused players from practice for farm work, deeming it as a suitable substitute for practice. Many of the coaches were farmers as well. The farm kids playing sports were resilient, physically and mentally strong from the farm life, and tough as a pine knots.

The College Grove High School football team in our inaugural season of 1973 had a perfect 10-0 win season. We went to the Class A State Football Play-offs only to lose to White House in the first round, with a score of 6-0. I was part of that team as a strapping one-hundred-twenty-five-pound freshman, but was certainly not an impact player. I continued to play football until I graduated from the first graduating class of Page High School in 1976.

Page High School was formed from the two small high schools of College Grove and Bethesda. Both College Grove and Bethesda schools had class sizes of twenty-five to thirty or less. My senior high school class of 1976 had a whopping one hundred and three graduates. My sister Lucy was the homecoming queen my senior year. I was honored to escort her onto the football field at halftime during the homecoming game as co-captain of the football team.

Lucy, homecoming queen, I'm #60. 1976.

When I lived in it, the home place was heated with wood by a potbellied stove in the kitchen—the large log room—and by three fireplaces: one in the main living room, one in the downstairs bedroom, and another in the upstairs bedroom.

Cutting wood to supply all the fireplaces was a necessity for heating the poorly insulated old house. We as a family, including the family dogs, all cut fire wood on a regular basis. *Oh, what fun!* Going to cut firewood was similar to a hay ride, only with wood instead of hay.

The old, grey *Major Diesel Ford* tractor was used to tow the wagon that hauled the firewood. Fallen trees were numerous on the farm from storms or decay, so we didn't have to cut many trees down. Loading the wood on the wagon didn't take long because we all pitched in and helped. All of us—including the dogs—jumped on and off the loaded wagon, both while it was stopped and while it was moving, never once thinking that one misstep could prove fatal.

My brother George and I roomed together in one of the upstairs bedrooms. The winter nights, upstairs and away from any of the fireplaces, proved to be downright frigid. It was not uncommon on many of the colder nights for George and me to see each other's breath as we talked. During the winter, I always slept with full pajama pants or sweat pants, sweat shirts, and long socks under many layers of blankets and quilts to keep warm.

The summertime nights were equally as challenging, only with the opposite problem—extreme heat. Even though the large beautiful maple trees in the front yard provided excellent shade, sometimes, on the hottest nights, the intolerable temperatures rivaled the hot summer nights at the cabin with Granddad.

I learned to handle the heat, but the red wasps nearly drove me crazy. More than once, I unknowingly crawled into bed with a wasp, only to be greeted with a sting on the leg or abdomen. I'm somewhat allergic to wasp stings. My body responds with an inordinate amount of swelling and redness. I soon learned to do bed checks for wasps as well as listen for the characteristic buzzing of a trapped wasp under the covers before climbing in. To this day, I hate red wasps.

My parents slept downstairs in the small bedroom next to the kitchen, separated by the small room/hallway that was once the dog trot. The sleeping quarters for myself and siblings were upstairs in two bedrooms: one bedroom for the boys, one bedroom for the girls.

The upstairs could be reached by going through the front porch hallway entrance, then up a beautiful cherry staircase with a landing. There was no way for us to sneak in late at night during our teenage years. Mom could hear the creaking of the cherry wood staircase as we tiptoed to our bedrooms and would holler out, "Is that you, George or Lucy or Charlie?"

At the back side of the boy's bedroom was a door leading to the attic. To me, the attic was extremely spooky. I don't know whether it was my vivid childhood imagination or if the attic was actually haunted, but strange noises could be heard coming from the attic. I was always scared to stay home by myself.

If the attic is haunted, it must be haunted with friendly ghosts, at least according to my niece. Jessica, who has Down syndrome, lives in the attic today. She says she has talked with my deceased father Abe and with Jesus. Jessica says, "Abe and Jesus are doing good and both say hi."

My parents

My father's typical farm attire was known far and wide as being a bit unusual. I really don't think he cared what people thought but wore what he thought was practical and comfortable. Dad had no idea what clothing matched what or what was in style, nor did it matter to him. His closet contained clothing spanning decades.

Dad was a sight to behold in his camouflaged Army pants, which he tucked into knee-high black socks and anchored with black lace-up Army boots. Completing the attire would be a long-sleeve, plaid shirt—winter or summer—and a wool sweater if it was cold. Dad acquired a pair of hot pink sunglasses from the Farmers Co-Op for a cattle pinkeye promotion and wore them with pride. He resembled a mole wearing glasses.

My mother's name is Jacqueline Price Hatcher. Of my parents, Mom was the disciplinarian, and her main tool for this purpose was the old wooden butter paddle. When appropriate, Mom would apply the butter paddle to our bottoms with such speed and precision that the paddle appeared not to be moving. Several licks were usually required to accomplish the full disciplinary effect. You could feel the sting on your back side inflicted by the paddle. The redness of the skin in the shape of the butter paddle was evident post paddling. It wasn't a good idea for the offending child to attempt to cover his or her butt to avoid the impact of the butter paddle, either. If attempted, his or her fingers and hands took the brunt of the force. The end result was bruised fingers instead of a bruised ego.

Both my parents believed in the importance of an education. Mom's lifelong love was and is music. She started early in life playing the piano and singing. She also has a keen appreciation of literature, poetry, and art. She says the strength in her fingers and hands was developed by hand-milking cows during her childhood. That acquired strength has come in quite handy when tickling the ivory.

Mom doing what she loves.

Mom obtained a bachelor's of science in music and advanced degrees in music education and choral directing. Three of the five of us kids could play a musical instrument. I think Jim and I were the only two who did not play an instrument. In those early years when we moved back to Tennessee, Mom taught music at the local high school, taught piano lessons on evenings and weekends, and directed the county choral society as well as fulfilling all the duties that raising five kids required.

Mom had a special ability to feed lots of people with a limited amount of food. She could take one whole baked chicken, seasoned to perfection, add some seasonal vegetables, and feed our family of seven plus anybody that was down on their luck at the time.

Dad inevitably would invite someone literally off the street to our home if he felt they were in need. He did this his whole life. It was not uncommon to have ten to twelve people total for dinner. Mom was raised by her parents with the memories of the Great Depression fresh on their minds, and was always very frugal with food and water, as well as being mindful of waste. Whatever food we put on our plates we were expected to consume entirely. Mom would even suck the chicken bones.

At the end of the Sunday dinner, at the center on the long kitchen table, the only remnants of the baked chicken would be a pile of bare, dry bones in the old, yellow, iron pot Mom used to bake the chicken. No skin, no gravy, and no meat would be left, yet I don't ever remember anyone going away hungry, even when it appeared to me when we started to eat that there wasn't enough food.

Lilly Mae, my African American nanny who greatly impacted my childhood years on the farm, helped my mother with all the child-care, cooking, and housework for over a decade. Lilly Mae resembled *Aunt Jemima*—the African American woman on the bottle of pancake syrup—in dress and appearance. She wore drab colored dresses, blouse tops, and a head wrap.

One of the housekeepers holding Cousin Paul.

Lilly Mae enjoyed smoking a pipe, and always smiled profusely when she was smoking. She was poor financially but surely not poor in spirit. She didn't drive, own a car or a house, or have many earthly possessions. Mom or Dad picked up Lilly Mae up at a tenant house some five miles away and brought her to our house to work. No one really knew how old Lilly Mae was. My dad helped Lilly Mae obtain a social security number after determining her approximate date of birth.

Lilly Mae acted as our mother in every respect in helping to raise us. She was as much a mother to us as Mom was during those very impressionable childhood years on the farm.

Although she wasn't really the kind of person that showed a lot of affection, we could tell she really loved us. She showed her love for us in many ways. She spanked us with switches from the willow tree by the spring in the front yard as needed without hesitation, but she also cooked for us, cleaned up after us, and washed our clothes. She also took us fishing.

Lilly Mae loved to go fishing in the large farm pond, which was within walking distance just up the road. Her bait of choice was either the big, green, plump worms (which she plucked off the sycamore leaves while the worms were still munching on them) or the glistening brown, almost purple, earthworms dug up from the manure-rich dirt from around the barns where the cattle lounged. Lilly Mae's favorite fishing pole was the very basic cane pole. She taught us how to tie the hook on the fishing line, how to bait the hook correctly, how to attach the red and white floats at the just the right depth to catch fish, and how to clean the fish we caught.

The farm pond was rich with plump blue gill that had colorful yellow and orange under-bellies, as well as with some bass and a few catfish. Lilly Mae's gift of love to us was a full country breakfast the next morning that included fresh fried fish battered in seasoned corn meal, fresh scrambled eggs— sometimes mixed with pork brains—and lard biscuits made from scratch. It was the breakfast of champions.

But the most important gifts from Lilly Mae were those life lessons of love. She taught us how to love and what it feels like to be loved, regardless of skin color, nationality, or material wealth. According to Lilly Mae, there is no distinction between black and white, only what she referred to as "peoples" created equally under God. I got a full view of this truth early on thanks to Lilly Mae. What a profound effect this good woman had on my life!

Chapter Seven

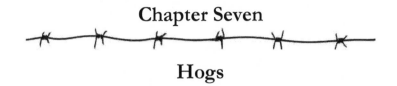

Hogs

The Hatcher home place in the curve of Arno Road was strategically placed beside a small babbling creek that runs through the farm. It's a convenient source of drinking water for people and livestock as well as an ideal source of running water for use during butchering time. The hog lot and hog barn that housed the eight to ten sows was located adjacent to the house, and the creek ran right through it.

Hogs in the field next to the homeplace.

The sows had baby pigs that were taken to a weight of forty pounds or more before being sold to other farmers as feeder pigs, where they would be fed out to a finished weight of two hundred pounds or more. Eight or ten of the feeder pigs were kept for us to feed out ourselves for hog killing in early winter. My father often fed the hogs something called slop. The recipe Dad used for slop was wheat shorts mixed with water in a large iron kettle. He didn't feed the hogs slop every day, but it was evident he liked feeding the hogs slop and that the hogs loved the slop. The slop was allowed to ferment till it was a sour, pungent brew.

Granddad with hogs in the granary lot.

When Dad said he was going to slop the hogs, what he meant was that he was going to feed the hogs slop. The slop was poured over the fence into a long wooden trough for the anxiously awaiting hogs to slurp up. By the time Dad poured the slop over the fence to the hogs, the hogs would be in such great anticipation of receiving the heavenly mixture that they would have worked themselves into a squealing feeding frenzy. As the slop was poured out, mayhem would quickly ensue as the hogs jockeyed for trough position. Soon, however, the squealing would stop. Nothing could then be heard but slurping and guzzling. Then it would be over. The trough would be empty, but looks of pure contentment would be obvious on the hogs' faces.

Corn was the mainstay of the hogs' diet. The corn was

stored in the old corn crib in the hog barn across the creek. To access the crib, one had to go through the four-foot access gate in the yard, enter the hog lot, cross the creek, cross the hog lot, open the latch on the corn crib door, and then hop into the crib.

One day in 1973, not long after moving to Tennessee, I was going into the corn crib when I noticed the initials CWH and the number 94 carved into a wide poplar board above the crib door. The carvings were the handy-work of Charles Wooldridge Hatcher, my grandfather's older brother, in the year 1894, when he would have been twenty-one. My natural response was to carve my initials—the same initials, CWH—and the number 73 for the year 1973 just below my namesake's into the same poplar board.

Just before the old dilapidated hog barn was torn down in the 1980's, I salvaged the old weather worn poplar board containing both CWH initials because of the tremendous sentimental value. The historic poplar board piece was placed over my back door porch frame in 1994 during the remodeling and construction of our log home, one hundred years after the original Charles Wooldridge Hatcher had left his mark. The inscriptions there today are a constant reminder to me of my Hatcher heritage on this farm every time I look up and see them as I enter the back porch door.

The shelled corn was kept in burlap sacks weighing one hundred pounds in the corn crib. Here was the challenge: if the hogs were hungry, and that was all the time, one needed to make it across the creek and through the hog lot to the corn crib cleanly without falling down or misstepping with the hogs in hot pursuit. I was convinced that if a person fell down in the hog lot, no remains would ever be found. Thus the hogs were affectionately known as killer hogs.

One day, I could hear Dad exclaiming loudly from across the creek near the hog barn, "Sons of bitches!" His fury echoed through the creek valley. Dad would occasionally cuss when he lost his temper, but he would never use the Lord's name in vain. He instilled that same thing in me. I was always scared that if I did use the Lord's name in vain, I would instantly be struck by lightning or worse. I have never wanted to test it out.

"Sons of bitches" was the worst thing Dad could come up with to say. I'm sure he had learned it from Granddad since Granddad used the phrase often and was apt to lose his temper more often than Dad. I also tend to say the same thing when I lose my temper. It's a generational thing, I guess. My inherited bad tendencies go along with the good.

When I heard Dad hollering, I knew what had happened. The group of old sows—killer hogs—he was feeding had grown impatient. If the shelled corn wasn't delivered to them fast enough, the hogs would be set off into a feeding frenzy like a bunch of piranhas with Dad as the bait. Thank goodness the killer hogs didn't take him to the ground or that would have been the end of him.

A moment later, Dad appeared in the home place yard via the side yard gate. Two bright-red blood spots were visible above his high, top-black army boots. One of the old sows had bitten him on the calf of his leg. The blood had seeped through his camouflaged pants and the tall black socks that the pants were tucked into. The two bloody spots matched exactly with the upper and lower incisors ("tushes") of the offending sow.

Dad went into the house. Mom, upon seeing Dad's wounds, was undaunted. She calmly attended to them, removing his left boot and sock, and then cleaning the jagged puncture wounds with soap and water. Dad didn't need sutures, but he did need a tetanus shot, necessitating a trip to town. When he returned to the farm, he went right back to work; it didn't slow him down a bit, and he worked the rest of the day like nothing ever happened.

Another hog-related episode at the same location had occurred many years earlier when my older sister Beth was a toddler. As the story goes, Beth was playing in the yard while Mom was hanging out clothes to dry on the clothes line. Out of the corner of her eye, Mom caught a glimpse of Beth in the hog lot, crawling gleefully toward the sows with baby pigs. I'm assuming Beth wanted to play with the baby pigs. If there is one thing a momma sow won't tolerate, it's messing with her baby pigs.

Mom realized Beth was in imminent danger. She sprinted toward the hog lot with no time to waste until she encountered the fence. There she transformed into part Olympic long jumper, part Olympic gymnast: vaulting the fence in a single bound as if launching off a spring board, she landed squarely on her feet on the hog lot side of the fence. The landing would have been scored a perfect ten in the Olympics. In one swift movement, she snatched up Beth in the nick of time, just before the sow, unimpressed, completed her furious charge. Beth was no worse for the incident.

The Great Hog Escapade: another disaster

I had learned my welding skills from my shop class at the old College Grove School, before the merger of College Grove School with Bethesda School formed Page High School. Feeling the need to try out my skills, I purchased a beat-up, two-horse trailer that needed some work. It was my intention to transform the horse trailer into a general livestock trailer to haul cattle and hogs to town when needed. All I had to do was remove the stall divider and weld the small tack access door, which was on the right hand side of the trailer, permanently shut. Or at least that's what I thought.

Mom agreed to go with me to Nashville to sell some hogs. She and I hooked up the freshly converted, rusty horse trailer—now hog conveyance—to our faded yellow, two-door, four-wheel-drive, beat-up *Toyota* farm truck. The *Toyota* truck was an excellent farm truck because it could maneuver the hills on the farm like a mountain goat. It could go anywhere on the farm, but it really wasn't made for pulling a trailer. We loaded up four old sows that had seen their better days to take to Nashville. I was feeling pretty good about my welding job as we headed toward Nashville with no premonition of what was about to occur.

Mom and I traveled uneventfully east on Interstate 40; traffic was brisk. We were just before the divide with Interstate 24 in downtown Nashville when I noticed people driving up alongside of us waving at us. I told Mom that it was real nice of them to be waving at us—then I looked into the passenger side truck mirror and in horror saw the flying hogs. That tack-access door that I had proudly welded was wide open and flopping in the wind. Two of the sows had jumped out of the trailer and were spinning like tops in the middle of Interstate 40. Cars and big trucks were swerving in and out to miss the hogs with horns blaring.

I feared the worst. Panic struck. My mind flashed to pictures of piles of overturned vehicles, dismembered hogs, and blood and guts. I slowed the truck and trailer down immediately but couldn't turn left toward the median because the traffic was intense. When I finally could pull over to the median, the trailer was completely empty; all the hogs had escaped.

My expectations were that all the hogs would be either dead or so badly damaged that they could not be sold. Much to my surprise, the four sows were up, grunting and moving about between the vehicles that were still traveling at high rates of speed; the hogs were seemingly oblivious to the present dangerous situation. The only visible evidence of the sows taking a spill on the roadway was the road rash strawberries the size of pie plates on the side of two of the sows.

A police car was headed towards us. I felt sure that he planned on assisting us. I was somewhat relieved until he just waved and drove off. I panicked again. How was I ever going to get these sows off Interstate 40, corralled, and loaded without harming man or beast? We happened to be right next to a housing project. Inhabitants of the community began to line up along the high chain link fence separating the project from the interstate as if a bunch of vultures waiting on their victims to die. I heard several exclaim, "Let's barbecue the hogs."

Fearing that all might be lost, I desperately surveyed the situation, praying there was some way to load the hogs. And then magically, things began to fall in place. The heavy, metal, bolted-together guard rails in the median formed a natural corral with a ten-foot opening facing due east. It was like the guard rails were installed from the beginning for the explicit purpose of loading these unfortunate sows on this particular day at this particular time.

Miraculously, one of the sows had already entered the guard rail corral. Two men had scaled the chain link fence, volunteering to assist in any way they could. Mom, myself, and the two volunteers used our hands and bodies at the sows' eye level to direct them, herding the remaining three sows into the guard rail corral as well. While the three of them stood guard at the corral opening, I quickly backed the truck and trailer into the opening, sealing off any escape routes for the sows.

My weld had broken loose on the side door, allowing the hogs to exit the trailer. I tied the side door securely shut with some baling twine I found in the bed of the *Toyota* truck and opened the trailer doors. The sows jumped on to the trailer without provocation. They must have been as anxious as we were to get the heck out of there.

The hogs were accepted at the slaughter house. There was no bruising of their meat. A check for the sows came in the mail a few days later. There was no mention of the adventure on the local evening news. All was well.

Hog castration

My brother George and I were summoned every spring to our good neighbor Mr. Douglas York's place to help with the castration of a group of his feeder pigs. Inevitably, Mr. York would wait too long before he called for assistance, thus allowing our patients to surpass a manageable size to be castrated easily.

I will have to admit it wasn't totally his fault. You see, it took many days of baiting the pigs into a stall to capture the little buggers because of the free-ranging nature of Mr. York's hog operation. The hogs literally had the run of the whole farm.

There was a log corn crib in the middle of the hog lot where Mr. York stored most of his corn. He did not shell the corn off the cob but chose to pick the whole ear with the corn on the cob. Mr. York pitched ears of corn to the awaiting hogs out of the corn crib. The older hogs had learned to eat the corn off the cob by skillfully rolling and holding the ears of corn to the ground with their feet. The younger pigs required extra protein, so Mr. York had his ear corn ground and mixed with soybean meal by the local feed mill owned by Robert White, our neighbor down the road.

Some of the pigs now weighed almost eighty pounds, about the same body weight as George and me. That's why we had to double-team them. The best way for us to handle pigs of this size was for George to grab one back leg and for me to grab the other, have both of us back into the corner of the stall, and present the ventral surface of the pig from that position to Mr. York to perform surgery.

The pig's front feet would in this way be firmly planted on the ground, the head of the pig dangling down with no restraint. As George and I would stand to either side of the pig, the pig was free to bite our ankles and calves at will. They always did, too, the sons of bitches, usually just as Mr. York was making his incision over the testicles or when he was stripping the testicles out. If Mr. York incised through the skin into the testicle just right, some sort of clear testosterone-laced, boar-smelling fluid would erupt from the shiny tunic covering of the testicles, sometimes squirting us in the face. Thank goodness I never got it in my mouth.

Upon completion of the procedure, purple or scarlet oil spray was copiously applied to the incision site. Since the pig would be kicking like a mule, George and I would also receive ample amounts of the spray on our hands and clothing as Mr. York attempted to apply the spray to a moving target.

Between the testicle juice and the fresh hog manure covering us, we would smell to high heaven for days. There was visual evidence of our pig encounter, too: our hands would be stained purple or red from the post-surgical spray. The smell and the bright stained colors were just something soap and water could not wash off our hands. It simply had to be worn off over time. For days when my eating utensils came to my mouth, I was reminded of the pig castration. I could smell it and see it on my hands. At church the following Sunday, George and I would sit on our hands on the back pew, hoping to stifle the aromatic and visual evidence of the York pig castration event.

Occasionally, there would be a pig in the group to be castrated that visibly bulged in the inguinal area. It was apparent as the pig walked. Mr. York called these pigs "bustled." They were actually pigs with inguinal hernias. If one castrated a pig with an inguinal hernia and didn't know it, the result was a heaping pile of intestines hanging out the castration incision. Not good! This happened a few times to us, so we learned that it's better to be aware that the pig has a hernia and be prepared.

Mr. York had learned to repair inguinal hernias using fishing line and a sewing needle. After incising the skin over the hernia, he bluntly dissected out the hernia pouch from surrounding · tissue, twisted the pouch until the intestines disappeared into the abdomen, and incorporated the remnants of the hernia pouch in the suture line of the inguinal ring. I used this same technique after I became a veterinarian.

Believe it or not, the testicles from the pigs were saved to be eaten. The outer tough covering of the testicles was removed, exposing the tender meaty pieces, and then washed thoroughly. The cleaned testicles were soaked in salt water overnight in the refrigerator. The next day, the meat pieces were rolled in seasoned corn meal batter and deep fried. We called this country delicacy, mountain oysters, which can either be pig testicles or calf testicles. I prefer pig testicles. The small-sized testicles are the tenderest and best to eat. I took mountain oysters to a church dinner one Sunday but didn't tell anyone what they were. There were no leftovers. At least two people commented to me that it was pretty good chicken.

Hog killing: serious business & good eating

The hogs on the farm were an important source of income as well as a necessary source of meat for everyone that lived or worked on the farm. When it came time for hog killing, all hands were on deck: Vernon Pagel, Sr., Vernon Pagel, Jr., Brimmage Tomlin, Douglas York, Lilly Mae, Mom, Dad, a few neighbors, and a handful of us kids.

Dad scheduled the hog killing when the weather man

forecasted three or four cold days in a row. Dad didn't want extremely cold days, just days with highs below forty-five degrees Fahrenheit, because he wanted the meat to cool but not freeze during the two day event.

Preparations for hog killing started a day or two before the actual event. A flat-bed wooden wagon, the large iron pots used for scalding, lard and crackling preparation, the hand-powered sausage grinder, and the knives—all had to be cleaned and positioned in just the right place. Dad laid in general supplies like cloth sausage bags, sausage seasoning, meat-wrapping paper, and sugar and salt—enough of everything to meet the needs for the number of hogs to be processed.

The first and worst part of the whole hog butchering process was the necessary step of killing the hog. If I could avoid this part, I did. The hogs selected to be killed were the ones that reached a body weight of between two hundred to two hundred fifty pounds. With so many people relying on the pork to feed their families going into the winter months, we generally processed eight to ten hogs.

We assembled the hogs chosen to be harvested in the lower stable of the hog barn just across the creek from the Hatcher home place. Vernon Pagel Sr. was the best shot with a gun, so he was generally the executioner. He used a twenty-two rifle to shoot the hogs at close range squarely between the eyes at a slightly downward angle, effectively stunning the hog and stopping brain function. After the rifle shot rang out, the hog would immediately drop lifeless to the ground, all four legs giving way at once.

It was important to cut or "stick" the throat of the hog, transecting the carotid arteries and the jugular veins, as soon as was practical so that all the blood would drain from the carcass. If the men working did not drain the blood quickly, there was a good chance the meat would be ruined because the blood would collect within the carcass, affecting the taste of the meat.

After the hog bled out, two or three men would work to attach the carcass by the Achilles heel of each back leg of the hog to a metal tree with two hooks on it. The metal tree was attached to a three-point hitch boom mounted on the back of the blue-bellied *Ford Dexter* tractor. Using the tractor, the carcass would then be moved to an awaiting large pot of boiling water and lowered it in for scalding. The scalding hot water loosened the hair. What hair didn't fall out, someone scraped off with the blades of large knives held perpendicular to the skin. Heaps of hog hair, black, white, red, and brown, accumulated in the bottom of the pot as the day went on.

The now-hairless carcass would be rinsed with cold water until clean. The importance of a sharp knife was much appreciated from this point forward. Whoever was in charge of the cutting removed the heads first and then, starting between the back legs, made an incision into the abdomen at the mid-line, being careful not to puncture any intestines all the way down to the diaphragm.

After trimming around the anus and rectum, the butcher—generally Vernon Sr. or Douglas York—would skillfully dissect all the intestines away from the back bone with care until they fell gently down together into awaiting galvanized tubs. Either an axe or pruning shears would be used to cut through the sternum to access the chest cavity. The contents of the chest cavity, including lungs and heart, would go into the galvanized tubs along with the intestines.

The overflowing galvanized tubs full of organs and intestines were taken down to Lilly Mae, who would be stationed strategically by the creek for cleaning. The cleansing of the intestines was a tedious job, as she had to open each piece to empty out all the intestinal content. Immersing the opened intestines into the gently flowing creek water aided the process of removal of debris and cleaning of the intestines.

Some people consider hog intestines, commonly called

chitlins by country folk, as a delicacy when properly cooked. I am not one of those people. I could never get over the smell and taste of chitlins no matter how much hot sauce was applied to them or how much alcohol was consumed. Chitlins can be boiled, fried, or grilled, but no manner of preparation is appealing to me. Some people like the organs: heart, lungs—called "lites" because they are air filled and float in water—kidneys, or liver to eat. To each his own, I suppose. Nothing went to waste from the entire hog killing process.

After a thorough cleaning of the headless, hairless carcasses, they would be delivered to the clean, wooden surface of the flat bed wagon. Douglas York and Brimmage Tomlin feverishly would go to work on the carcasses with their freshly sharpened knives, dividing each carcass into quarters. The quarters and heads of the hogs were placed on the tin roof of the red shed to be cooled overnight. The cutting and deboning process is easier after the carcass has cooled. They were also placed on the roof to prevent predators from stealing the meat overnight. It was an unnerving sight to see all those hog heads sitting in a row on top of the roof. The day's work was so exhausting that we would have no trouble sleeping soundly that night.

The next morning, we would further divide the quartered carcasses into various cuts depending on what was requested. The most requested cuts were back strip—the most tender part of the whole hog—bacon, whole hams, and bone-in or boneless roasts. The fresh cuts of meat requiring no salt curing or seasoning were wrapped like Christmas presents, except without a bow, in plain white wax paper. Any meat pieces/parts that didn't fall into select cuts were cubed and placed in big metal pans to be hand ground into either fresh ground pork (unseasoned) or fresh ground sausage (seasoned).

The great thing about the second morning of processing was that we got to sample the sausage after Mom cooked it; she made sure that it achieved just the right amount of sage, salt, red and black pepper, and other seasonings. The repeated tasting required to achieve this perfection meant that we had to eat a lot of sausage, but somebody had to do it.

Douglas York trimming hog meat.

The hand-turned sausage grinder that was mounted on the side of the wagon extruded the sausage into flour-coated sausage sleeves made out of cotton. Mom used the flour so that the sausage wouldn't stick to the insides of the sleeves so tightly, allowing the sleeves to fill with sausage much more easily. The sausage sleeves were hung with grass baling twine on nails in the smoke house. At this point, the sausage was ready either to eat or to be smoked with hickory wood in the smoke house for several days if desired.

Another one of Douglas York's hog-killing duties was for him to make souse or head cheese from all the various pieces/parts of the hog head except for the brains. He made souse because he liked it. I was never fond of souse, although with enough pepper added I could choke it down. Once Mr. York had removed the brains from the hog heads, Mom would mix the brains with fresh eggs and fried them up. We always ate them up readily with all that pork sausage that was being sampled—a great breakfast indeed.

Under the skin of a properly finished hog is a fairly thick layer of fat. The fat would be sliced up into cubes and taken to Lilly Mae. Lilly Mae would have a roaring fire going under a large iron pot near the maple tree by the garage. The skin and fat pieces, as well as any fat anywhere else on the carcass, would be pitched into the hot pot. The heat liquefied all the solid fat so that it could be poured into five-gallon tin lard stands. The lard was a beautiful creamy white when it solidified after cooling down. Everyone knows a biscuit made with lard is the best. Today, we are beginning to learn that lard is a good fat.

Lilly Mae cooking cracklings.

The skin and fat cubed pieces reduced down to tasty morsels called cracklings. These weren't store-bought, processed cracklings; these were real cracklings. They were best eaten warm right out of the pot when the fat globules burst with flavor in your mouth. The fat ran down our cheeks both inside and out. We ate cracklings as snacks through the winter months like potato chips.

My dad and Sharon cooking cracklings.

Thinking back on it now, I wonder how in the world we could consume that much fat. I know the answer. For one thing, this wasn't processed fat; for another, we worked like Trojans all day long. The fat was our fuel—energy. We burned it up as we worked. We had very active lives on the farm in those days, and still do.

The hams are from the top portion of the rear legs. True country hams are salted; whole city hams are sugar-cured. We rubbed a white powder called Borax onto the sawed-off and exposed bone of the ham to prevent cut worm penetration. The hams were massaged and coated with a curing mixture consisting of plain white salt, brown sugar, and saltpeter (potassium nitrate), then placed in a salt box. The ham and salt were alternated in layers until all the hams were appropriately covered with a goodly amount of salt.

Cousin Bill surveying the meat.

After a couple of days, we would remove the hams, inspect them, wrap them in brown paper, and place them in a hanging net bag. We would use an ice pick to drive a hole through the neck of the ham, then use old recycled baling wire to fashion a hook to hang the hams up in the smoke house. The hams hung beautifully in the smoke house like upside-down lollypops.

Every month, Dad would inspect them for insect or rodent assault. The hams stayed in the smoke house, growing tastier every day until early the next fall. The hams were good almost indefinitely after curing, although they would shrink down to almost half their original size. No wonder our forefathers liked salt curing meats in the days before refrigeration. The end result was tasty meat for months to come.

When removing a ham from the smoke house after it was cured, one almost always found a nice green, white, and blue mold covering it. However, the ham was perfectly good; all you had to do is scrape the mold off and you were good to go.

Granddad once sent a country ham to some city folk friends up North. They promptly discarded the ham, thinking it was bad because it was covered in mold. What a waste!

There is nothing better than country ham cooked in a black iron skillet, served in a pool of red-eye gravy, just as Granddad made at the cabin during our summers with him. I like to saturate good lard biscuits with red eye gravy. Now that's good. You get your monthly allowance of salt in one meal.

Dad distributed the meat from the hog killing to all those on the farm and all those that helped with the hog-killing process. Some meat was also given to those in the community in need. Hog killing was just another way that the farm gave back.

**It's me carrying a ham;
note the old Blue *Montego* in the background.**

Chapter Eight

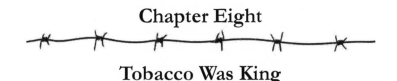

Tobacco Was King

Raising tobacco on the farm was similar to killing hogs in that everyone who participated benefited from it. Vernon Pagel Sr., Vernon Pagel Jr., Brimmage Tomlin, my brother-in-law Bill, my brother George, and myself all derived income based on our level of participation on our farm.

The first year I helped with the tobacco, I made seven hundred dollars. With each successive year, I earned more until I reached a maximum of around two thousand. I used some of the money to go on two high school trips to Europe and put the rest toward college tuition.

Our good neighbor, Douglas York, raised tobacco on his place as well. As good neighbors do, we helped each other in tobacco and hay when needed. In our area, most farmers raised burley tobacco, not the dark-fired tobacco that required being smoke cured within the tobacco barn. I would later be exposed to dark-fired tobacco in Kentucky when we moved there for my second veterinary job.

Tobacco is one of those crops that take a tremendous amount of physical labor and planning. Almost everything was done by hand. In many ways it is much harder than raising hay. Preparation of the seed bed starts in the very early spring. We located the seed beds and the tobacco patch based on good soil fertility and the ability of the soil to drain ground water.

The seed beds were always in close proximity to the tobacco patch so we wouldn't have to haul the tobacco seedlings or slips very far. Tobacco grows best in rich, well-drained soil. We broke (plowed) and disked the ground until it was as smooth as a baby's butt.

The outside temperature would still be cold when we gassed the beds, using canisters of extremely toxic chemicals— now banned—to prevent the growth of noxious weeds. After strategically placing trays containing the gas canisters in the seed beds, we would cover them with black plastic. The trays had sharp metal protruding points in them that punctured the canisters of gas when someone applied downward pressure from outside of the plastic. We would remove the plastic when early spring came, sow tobacco seed in the seed beds, and then cover the beds again with see-through, netting-like material which allowed moisture and sunlight to penetrate.

By May, a nice uniform bed of tobacco slips would be present after we removed the netting. We pulled the tobacco slips up, roots and all, from the tobacco beds to be transplanted to the tobacco patch. We prepared the tobacco patch ground for the fledgling tobacco slips in the same manner as the beds, but not to the same extent.

The laborious process of "pulling the slips" had to be done on the same day transplanting took place or the tender tobacco plants would not survive. On tobacco slip transplanting day, work always began as the sun came up. There wasn't any easy way to pull slips. Pulling slips required you to bend all the way over or get down on your hands and knees for hours in order to provide enough slips to transplant or set for the day. Armfuls of slips were wrapped in bundles using pieces of burlap sacks. The bundles were open on each end with the roots all in one direction. Short pieces of number-nine wire tightly secured the burlap sacks around the bundles of slips, similar to diaper pins securing a diaper on a baby.

Mr. Pagel was the most skillful tractor driver and drove the blue-bellied *Dexter Ford* tractor, which pulled the old tobacco setter, once steel-wheeled and mule drawn but later converted to tractor-drawn. His rows were straight and true. The tobacco setter was a one-row setter with two hard, unpadded, metal seats. One person who possessed good hand-eye coordination, usually one of us kids, would sit in each seat with a bundle of tobacco slips in our laps.

Mr. Douglas York

The object was for each person to alternately, but simultaneously, place one tobacco slip at a time into the groove that the setter had created in the soil. Each time the setter made a clicking noise, a burst of water would bathe the slip as the wheels on each side of the groove packed the loose soil around the slip. There was a chance that the person placing the slip in the groove between the wheels at the same time as a rock passed through could have their fingers mashed. The severity was dependent on the size of the rock. Fingers were not mashed often, but every setter that spent any time riding the tobacco setter had experienced a hand injury.

For the next several days, we would watch the fledgling tobacco slips closely for survival. When slips did not make it, we would replant the space by making a hole in the ground with a peg (short wooden stick), being careful that the slip was perpendicular to the ground and pointing directly to the sky.

Weed control in the tobacco patch was a big deal. If weeds were not controlled, the competition for soil nutrients greatly diminished the tobacco crop. Chopping weeds out by hand with hoes in the sweltering summer was an all-day, everyday occurrence for some time.

Keeping a hoe sharp was very important. We always carried files in our back pockets for sharpening our hoes. Working with a dull hoe requires more effort to chop the weeds and intensifies the blisters on the palms of his hands. A good pair of work gloves is a must when chopping weeds in a tobacco patch, although wearing those does not entirely guarantee not getting any blisters. I can remember popping the blisters with a needle, erupting clear fluid from them. Removal of the dead white skin with my teeth revealed a layer of fiery red, unprotected, and painful skin.

We were fortunate enough to have a very small and lightweight *Allis Chalmers* tractor equipped with hand-controlled small plows we called the "chicken scratcher." We would use the chicken scratcher to plow the weeds down between the rows of tobacco once the weeds defeated our hoeing capabilities. Although the chicken scratcher was pretty effective in plowing up the weeds between the rows, the least damaging way of mechanical weed control was by a well-trained mule or team of mules. By the late '70's, the days of using mules and draft horses for farm work, at least for non-Amish farmers, were coming to an end. However, at that time we still had a pair of bay mules named Maude and Jane.

Brimmage Tomlin was the one on the farm that knew best how to harness, hook up, and work Maude and Jane. He had done it all his life and was the mules' caretaker. Mr. Tomlin, Maude, and Jane were all nearing retirement, but they worked at the same slow steady pace, had the same good work ethic, understood each other, and generally worked well as a team.

Mr. Brimmage Tomlin on the left, cousins in the center, and Vernon Pagel Sr. on the right.

The mule barn was the barn on top of the hill next to the tobacco barn. It had two stalls, a tack room, a hay loft, and sheds on both sides. Both sheds had hay racks for feeding square bales of hay to the livestock. Mr. Tomlin equipped Maude first and then Jane, placing the bridles with blinders, yokes, harnesses, long reins and all necessary equipment for plowing weeds on the mules with care. After attaching the weed plow to the mules, Mr. Tomlin, Maude, and Jane would then head off to the tobacco patch with the plow on its side in transport mode.

Mr. Tomlin was getting up in his years. It took exceptional strength and finesse for anyone to handle a pair of mules and to manipulate the plow in and out of the ground, but there was Mr. Tomlin at an advanced age somehow getting it done. One of the many lessons I learned from Mr. Tomlin was just that: do hard physical work as long as you can despite your age.

Maude and Jane pulled the plow at a rapid pace and Mr. Tomlin always had trouble keeping up. He took big, arching, stilted steps, wavering from side to side like the scarecrow in *The Wizard of Oz* to keep up. I only saw him fall once. He quickly picked himself up, briefly dusted himself off, and continued.

Mr. Tomlin would issue Maude and Jane verbal commands, mixing in expletives when necessary. "Gee", "Whoa," "I mean Whoa," and other words echoed through the hills and valleys. At the end of the day, the tobacco patch would be pristine—not a weed could be seen. Maude, Jane, and Mr. Tomlin would be all lathered up with sweat, tired to the bone. They had put in an honest day's work. I really admired them for the hard work that they had done. Maude, Jane, and Mr. Tomlin then would head back to the mule barn for an evening of much needed rest, only to repeat the process the very next day at Douglas York's place.

There was a mutual gained respect between Mr. Tomlin and his mules. Mr. Tomlin respected the mules for the long, hard day's work that they gave him, and the mules respected Mr. Tomlin for the care and admiration that he gave them. Mr. Tomlin's respect for the mules was so great that he often told me, "Son, always do all a mule can do." I think what he meant was to give it all you've got, and work as hard as you can and as long as you can, as good mules do. When you do that, good things will come to you in life.

Besides weeding, tobacco plants also needed to be topped. It was while I was doing just this that I experienced one of two episodes of being very ill while working with tobacco. Ironically enough, I had my just had my wisdom teeth pulled at the time. I didn't show much wisdom the day I got sick. I should have known better. My wisdom teeth were pulled in the morning, and I worked in the tobacco patch the same evening.

Topping is the removal of the bloom on the top of the tobacco plant by snapping the bloom off by hand or cutting it off with a pocket knife. The tobacco plant would produce much larger leaves after topping, and the leaves were what we were after.

The heat, the seepage of blood from the holes in my jaw, and the subsequent swallowing of blood made me intensely nauseous. As the sun began to set, my stomach began to churn. I spewed volcanic spurts of vomit in the tobacco patch until my stomach was empty. I had the dry heaves until I succumbed to sleep later that night. I did learn a valuable lesson, though: don't go to the tobacco patch after having your wisdom teeth pulled.

Once the tobacco reached maturity, it was harvested or cut on what always seemed like the hottest day in August. It never failed. There are various ways to cut tobacco, but the fastest way for us was to cut and pile five stalks at a time. The serious tobacco worker was like an artist and had his own equipment: a tobacco knife/hatchet to cut the tobacco and a tobacco spear to spear the tobacco. The fastest person I ever saw cut and spear tobacco was Vernon Pagel Jr. He was machine-like, cutting tobacco down so fast it seemed like a hay mower was doing it.

We drank a lot of water on those hot, humid Tennessee days. The tobacco rows seemed endless at times. We longed for the end of the rows because we knew we could stop and lounge in the shade of the fence row or under the wagons, gulping water from our five-gallon water coolers.

The piles of five tobacco plants were speared onto one-by-two-inch oak tobacco sticks that were three feet long. One end of the tobacco stick was placed in the ground upright, and a tobacco spear was placed on the other end of the stick. This would put the top of the spear nearly chest high. Each tobacco plant had to be raised up onto the spear near the end and center of the tobacco plant and thrust downward, threading it onto the tobacco stick all in one motion. This was repeated until at least five plants were on a stick. This motion was better for muscle building than any arm workout in any gym. It resulted in muscular forearms and shoulders on all participants. This was one of the reasons that both Vernon Pagel Sr. and Jr. were so strong.

By the end of the day, our arms and shoulders would ache. We'd flip the last plant over to the side, where it acted as a prop to hold the completed stick upright off the ground. Once the tobacco was cut, it was left it in the field for a day or two to cure. It was then either loaded and stacked by hand onto a flatbed wagon or hung it on tobacco wagons designed for that purpose.

Rain or dirt splashing up on the already cut tobacco plants from the rain was not good. Not only did it affect the quality of the tobacco leaves when they were sold, but it also made the loading, unloading, and hanging of the tobacco much more unpleasant. Any extra moisture or soil on the tobacco made the work harder and dirtier. So, not unlike when making hay, we looked at the weather forecast prior to cutting tobacco to avoid the rain.

The loads of cut tobacco were hauled to the five-acre tobacco barn on the hill. Granddad had built the barn in the early 1960's from oak timber cut off the farm. The barn was magnificent, a state of the art tobacco barn for that day and time. The barn still stands proudly today on the hill despite a rusty tin roof and frayed wooden siding. It now houses hay and farm equipment, not tobacco.

The tobacco barn on the hill when it was first built.

A tobacco barn is basically a pole barn with four-by-four-inch-square oak boards in tiers about three to three-and-a-half feet apart. The center section of the barn had five tiers at the tallest part. The tiers were about around eight feet apart. That's equivalent to a five or six-story building.

I'm scared of heights, so hanging tobacco in the upper tiers was a real challenge for me. The tobacco wagon was pulled as close as possible to the section of the barn we were hanging tobacco on. Both Mr. Tomlin and Mr. York had the responsibility of unloading the tobacco off the wagon because they could stand on the ground and pass the full tobacco sticks to the next person without fear of falling. The most nimble and dispensable of the kids were designated as the top tier barn attendants, straddling precariously across the span of the four-by-four square poles at the top of the barn.

Mr. Pagel would be on the first tier—he handled every tobacco stick—Vernon Jr. on the second tier, my brother George on the third tier, myself on the fourth tier, and my sister Lucy at the very top of the barn. The fully-loaded, heavy tobacco sticks were passed between our legs in front of our bodies overhead to the next person above us in assembly line fashion for placement on their respective tier or tiers. We had no safety equipment or straps, absolutely nothing to break our fall if we fell. I can't imagine my grandson at the top of the barn today.

The tobacco sticks loaded with the plants on them were passed successively to the awaiting hands of those of us up in the barn. It was assumed the person above you would do their job and you would not be knocked out of the barn by a falling bunch of tobacco. Hanging tobacco in the barn was a test of balance, strength, and coordination as we perched like birds on a wire in the barn handling the weight of the tobacco sticks. This served me well years later when I took gymnastics in college.

We hung the sticks across the four-by-four oak poles starting at the top and working our way down to the bottom. This process was repeated load after load, stick after stick, and top to bottom until the five-acre-capacity barn was full. It wasn't so bad being at the top of the barn, even though it was more dangerous because you didn't handle as many sticks. I often wondered what would happen if one of us had fallen out of the barn, but, thank goodness, it never happened.

I got sick a second time from working in tobacco on one fall night the last year that we completely filled Granddad's tobacco barn. A light shower came one late afternoon and rained on about a half-acre of tobacco we had already cut. The next day we loaded the tobacco after the sun had dried out the outside leaves.

I wore a sleeveless shirt that day. Apparently, during the day while I was hanging tobacco, nicotine-laced rain water from the inside tobacco leaves dripped onto my bare arms. The nicotine must have been absorbed through my skin and entered my blood stream, giving me nicotine poisoning. I became violently ill that night, sweating and vomiting. I thought I was going to die. It was similar to the time when I got sick at eight years old when I smoked a half a pack of cigarettes in the tree house. I never smoked another cigarette after that day in the tree house, and that prohibition was reinforced this night as well.

When we finished hanging all our tobacco, we weren't quite done yet. Oh, no! Douglas York had helped us get up our tobacco, and now we had to help him get up his. Mr. York didn't have nearly as much tobacco as we had, so it didn't take long. However, his tobacco barns were not like the state-of-the-art tobacco barn structure that Granddad had built. These barns were rickety sheds in a poor state of repair. The barn poles to hang the tobacco on were round farm cut six inch saplings thrashed to the barn beams by used baling twine or wire.

George, Lucy, Vernon Jr, and I had an awful time just standing on the saplings, much less trying to handle the tobacco sticks. The poles would roll and sway under our feet as we worked. It was good training for skiing moguls on a black diamond ski slope. If that wasn't bad enough, fire bomb attacks from red wasps or bumble bees caused us to bail out of our positions in the barn many times until the offenders were doused with gasoline.

Usually, though, we got through it all somehow unscathed. Mr. York's tobacco crop and our crop were then safely in the barn.

Vernon Pagel Sr. in the tobacco patch.

Tobacco stripping in January

One year, in the mid to late '70's, we had a bumper crop. We didn't finish hanging all the tobacco until late fall, thus delaying the stripping of the tobacco until December. All the local tobacco warehouses where our tobacco was normally sold closed on the last day of December. Ordinarily we were finished stripping by this time and were able to sell our crop locally. That year was different. Once stripping was complete, the crop had to be hauled to a tobacco warehouse in Kentucky to be sold where warehouses were still open.

About this time, my oldest sister Beth had married, adding my new brother-in-law Bill to the farming operation. Bill brought many assets to the farming operation, including his mechanical prowess—much needed on any farm—and a ragtop, 4-wheel-drive, big-tired, yellow *Jeep*—also much needed. In order to strip tobacco, which means to remove the tobacco leaves from the plant, the tobacco first had to come "in case." "In case" means that the tobacco leaves had to become soft and pliable so that when stripping was performed the leaves would not shatter or tear. Moisture has to be in the air before tobacco will come "in case." There is nothing like a good, high-moisture weather front coming into the area; either snow or rain can do this. On one cold January day of this particular winter, snow was in the forecast, and as the front started to move within our area, the tobacco hanging in the barn came "in case."

When this occurred, all hands were summoned: Mr. York, Mr. Tomlin, Vernon Sr., Vernon Jr., Bill, and myself. The tobacco was removed from the sticks, piled, and covered with tarps to keep it "in case." We began the stripping—pulling the leaves off the stalk by hand—all of the tobacco in the stripping room. Attached to the tobacco barn, the stripping room was equipped with a very large oak table to grade the tobacco on, three overhead fluorescent lights, and a potbellied stove to keep us warm.

The six of us were broken up into two teams of three each. We stripped the tobacco leaves and placed them into one of three grades: bottom leaves, middle leaves—bright—and tips. The leaves of each grade were accumulated into a large handful and then wrapped at the base with a folded, four-inch-broad, tobacco leaf, securing the leaves into what was called a "hand." The graded hands were hung on a tobacco stick protruding out from the oak table parallel to the ground at waist level.

Periodically throughout the day, Mr. Tomlin would select what he thought was a tasty tobacco leaf, put it in his mouth and begin to chew. He would have the same look on his face as a contented cow does when chewing her cud. I tried doing the same thing one day and had to spit out the mouthful of tobacco because I was on fire. I do not know how Mr. Tomlin stood it. At the end of the day, Mr. Pagel had skillfully stacked all the hands by grade by into mounds six feet tall.

The predicted impending front did come soon after we finished the stripping that night dumping four to six inches of the most beautiful pure white snow I had ever seen on the farm. My brother-in-law Bill picked me up the next morning in his old *Jeep* to continue stripping tobacco on the hill. The *Jeep* was equipped with a rag top, but on this blistery cold January day, the rag top was not in place.

The roads were snow-covered and in poor driving shape, but we had no problem making our way to Mr. Tomlin's house back in the hollow to pick him up. However, once we had made it up the steepest part of the driveway going up on the hill, we started encountering problems. On the flat part of the ridge, a strong north easterly wind had drifted the snow level with the sloped upper bank of the driveway up above the level of the front bumper of the *Jeep*.

Bill was driving, Mr. Tomlin was in the front passenger side seat, and I was in the back jump seat. We were all dressed for the weather. Bill and I had on insulated coveralls, gloves, and toboggans (stocking hats). Mr. Tomlin had on multiple clothing layers: a frayed, insulated, blue-jean farm coat, gloves, and one of those fuzzy hats with ear flaps like the one the flying squirrel wears in *The Rocky & Bullwinkle Show*.

As we entered the snow bank, the bottom of the *Jeep* began to become wedged, forcing us to a stop. The four-wheel drive didn't seem to help. Bill repeatedly went from reverse to forward first gear, ramming the snow bank with all four wheels spinning, but we could not advance. Mr. Tomlin was holding on for dear life to the handle on the *Jeep* dash directly in front of him, stiff armed, bracing himself for impact, as good as an all-pro NFL running back could do.

Every time Bill made a run at the snow bank, the momentum would rock Mr. Tomlin back and forth, raising the unbuttoned fuzzy ear flaps on his hat each time. This happened over and over again until we finally gave up and went home. No tobacco stripping was done that day.

That year, stripping the tobacco crop was completed by the end of January after all the local tobacco warehouses had closed. It was early spring when Mr. Pagel drove the big old *International* farm truck, fully loaded with tobacco, to the warehouse in Kentucky. It was our largest tobacco crop to date and one of our last. We quit raising tobacco a few years later.

Chapter Nine

Lessons from the Older Generation

Even when Mr. Tomlin, Mr. York and my granddad were all advanced in years, I was continually amazed at their ability and willingness to do hard physical labor so late in life. Hard work may have been the key to their longevity, keeping them healthy even though their meals were riddled with high levels of unprocessed animal fat from foods like lard, bacon, sausage, biscuits, whole milk, whole cream, and eggs. This is totally contrary to what many say today, but the difference between then and now is that most of us don't work as hard as they did virtually every day of their lives.

Mr. Tomlin

Mr. Tomlin was a perfect example that hard work can be done at any age. He was relentless when packing a fence post. Mr. Tomlin could pack posts using a heavy steel tamping rod all day long without stopping. He wasn't fast but was extremely persistent and paced himself. His endurance much exceeded mine.

Mr. Tomlin was a very wise old man. His wisdom was not gained by formal education but rather by life itself. He was a patient person, too, well suited for raking hay and for being my fencing and tobacco mentor. Both required a tremendous amount of patience.

His usual wardrobe included blue faded coveralls, a narrow-brimmed straw hat, and brown, ankle-high, lace-up brown boots. If he wanted to dress up, Mr. Tomlin would wear a new pair of dark blue coveralls. He always knew what time it was; he carried a shiny silver pocket watch in the front of his coveralls in the pocket made for a pocket watch. The wind-up pocket watch kept perfect time. Oh, how times have changed—I don't even carry a watch of any type these days because I use my smart phone as my time keeper.

When Mr. Tomlin smiled, the smile revealed only a few teeth. A lifetime of chewing tobacco had taken its toll. Most days he was seen with a day or two's worth of beard growth and a chew of tobacco in his mouth. When he did shave, the nicks on his face and neck inflicted by the straight razor were noticeable because of the blood-tinged pieces of toilet paper used to control the bleeding.

Mr. Tomlin's chewing tobacco of choice was *Red Ox*, which was the strongest chewing tobacco that I knew of. Even just a little bit of it would make me gravely ill, but Mr. Tomlin could chew it and swallow the juice with no ill effects. It wasn't uncommon for a little trail of tobacco juice to be running down his chin. I had tremendous respect for him. He had done more work in his life and knew more about raising tobacco and fencing than I ever will.

Some of the most important and useful things I have learned in life are the simple ones. For example, Mr. Tomlin taught me that proper fencing begins with post selection. The longest lasting fence post far and away that was abundantly available to us was the locust post. Locust wood is hard and durable against the elements. Over time, the wood becomes so hard that one can't nail a fence staple into the post without bending the staple. There are many locust posts on our farm today that were put in the ground over fifty years ago.

Mr. Tomlin prided himself in being able to put a post in the ground that would not move. The entire time he was packing the post, he would test the tightness in the ground by pushing the post slightly with his hand. There is nothing worse than a fence with a bunch of wobbly posts in the ground, resulting in a loose fence.

Mr. Tomlin taught me that when putting a fence post in the ground, you should put the big end of the post or the end with a knot on it in the ground first. Then a mixture of rock and dry dirt must be packed in continuously all the way to the top of the hole until the post is as solid a bed rock. This seems simple enough, but it really makes a difference in the durability of a fence.

Besides putting in fence posts that don't move and are solidly in the ground, the next most important thing to making a good fence is the proper construction of the brace posts, whether they are the corner posts or the posts along long stretches or turns of the fence. Mr. Tomlin always used the thick but malleable number-nine brace wire when bracing fence posts.

First, he would use a chain saw to make a place to put the ends of the brace posts in each fence post. Then the resulting notches were chipped out cleanly with an axe. The brace post would then be placed into the awaiting etched-out places in the fence posts and secured in place by long nails driven through the brace post and into the fence post at an angle. The number-nine wire was wrapped around the top of one fence post and the bottom of the other fence post, then was drawn tight. Mr. Tomlin would make cedar wood pieces—three inches by three inches by two feet long—to tighten the number-nine wire. By placing the cedar sticks between the two strands of wire and twisting, the wire could be made as tight as a banjo string.

In those days, we used fifty-two-inch high woven wire with a strand of barb wire on top as our fencing material of choice. Today, we use high tensile wire because it can be tightened if loosened up by a falling tree or rampant cow. Otherwise, after all these years not much has changed when it comes to fencing on our farm. The fencing lessons taught to me by Mr. Tomlin some forty years ago are as relevant today as when he showed me the first time.

My brother-in-law Bill and I headed out one day to Robinson Hill, the northern-most part of the farm, to try out the fencing skills we had learned from Mr. Tomlin. Robinson Hill, now called Abe's Mountain, was the property of about one hundred acres that my father purchased when he was a young man. It's one of the tallest hills in Williamson County if not the tallest. It's the same piece of property where my granddad was bitten by the fox and where the beef barn was located.

The beef cows had been getting out on the back side of Robinson Hill over onto the neighbor's land. Bill and I planned to repair the fence. We had hooked the old grey *Major Diesel Ford* tractor to an ancient old, nonfunctional manure spreader—now used just to haul things—that was loaded with heavy locust posts, barbed wire, post-hole diggers, and other supplies needed to repair the fence.

The winding wagon trail going up the south side of the hill once used by my forefathers to travel to Franklin, Tennessee, was the best way to the top. We arrived at the top in good shape with Bill driving the tractor and myself sitting on the right fender. Then, as we proceeded to descend the steepest decline of the back side of the hill to where the fence was down, trouble ensued. The tires of the old *Major Diesel* began to slip on the grass, sliding at first, then scooting, picking up speed as we went.

Bill hollered over his shoulder, "Do you think we should jump?"

I replied, "Yes, but I'm not jumping until you do."

I saw Bill's blue-jean coverall butt disappear over the left fender well of the tractor out of the corner of my eye. That was my cue; I took a swan dive off the side of the tractor, being careful to clear the path of its right rear tire so I wasn't smashed like a bug. I hit the ground at a roll, tumbling down the side of the hill like a stuntman. Everything appeared to me in slow motion as I went upright and then upside down. I figured it was better to roll and adsorb the impact rather than hit the ground with a thud, possibly shattering bones. When I finally came to a stop after rolling a good twenty yards down the hill, I gathered my senses. My first concern was for Bill. Had he survived the fall? I frantically scanned the hillside, adrenalin pumping, with that same sick feeling in my stomach I had felt previously a few times in my life when tragedy struck, until I saw Bill. He was brushing the accumulated grass, leaves, and dirt off his backside with his hands. I breathed a big sigh of relief.

When we realized we were both okay, Bill and I turned our attention to the *Major Diesel*, now headed unattended on a one-way collision course with a large hackberry tree in the fence row at the bottom of the hill. We began to run downhill as fast as we could on the steep terrain in hopes of mounting the runaway tractor and averting the impending collision. We didn't make it. The old *Major Diesel* hit the tree squarely with a loud crash of splintering tree and twisting tractor metal. Neither the tractor nor the tree gave an inch.

The tires of the old *Major Diesel* were still spinning against the tree to no avail when Bill mounted the tractor to disengage it. Surprisingly enough, damage was minimal. The tree had a large gash in it at the level of the *Major Diesel's* heavy steel-front grill, exposing the white inside of the trunk. The front grill of the tractor was bent and somewhat mangled, but not severely enough to damage the radiator. The old *Major Diesel*, strong and proud, was still fully functional.

As fate would have it, the crash site was within ten yards of the escape route of the beef cows onto the adjoining neighbor's property. The border fence, which was comprised of multiple strands of old rusty barb wire lashed between two trees, was ridden down to ankle height. The hair from the Hereford cows that were crossing the wire was evident in the barbs. Fortunately, this time Bill and I didn't have to use our Mr.

Tomlin fence-post packing prowess. We quickly repaired the fence by re-stretching the existing barb wire at the proper height between the existing trees. This was a good thing because we weren't ready for an all-out fencing repair, being all bruised up from the traumatic tractor episode. Battered but not broken, the old *Major Diesel*, Bill, and I descended the front face of Abe's Mountain, never again to return to that steep western slope.

Mr. York

By the late 1970's, times were changing: Mr. Pagel and family had already left to work at another dairy, Mr. Brimmage Tomlin was not in good health, and Mr. Douglas York's wife had passed away. The older generation that I had learned so much from was beginning to go away.

Mr. York was not taking the passing of his wife very well. All his adult life, she had been there for him. She had cooked for him, washed his clothes, and kept the house looking like the house in *Hansel and Gretel* his entire married life. Now she was gone. He was alone in the rock house at the end of Nathan Smith Road with nothing to think about but the necrotic worsening spider bite that he had acquired a few weeks before.

The doctors were telling him that the amputation of the affected leg was eminent. The black and draining spider bite wound was causing his leg to swell to twice its normal size. We didn't realize the extent of the depth of depression Mr. York had fallen into until it was too late. He was in a big black hole and he couldn't climb out. The grim reality of his present state was too much for him to bear without his lifelong love.

Our mailman, Mr. Butts, while delivering mail to Mr. York early one fateful morning, discovered a note in Mr. York's mail box. It simply read, "Mr. Butts please come in the house." My brother-in-law Bill and I were headed into the hollow on Nathan

Smith Road in the old, beat-up *Toyota* truck when we noticed Mr. Butt's mail car rapidly approaching us in a cloud of dust. When he reached us and had pulled up side by side, out of breath, he hollered out the car window in a trembling voice, "Mr. York has killed himself." Mr. Butts told us that he had already called the sheriff from the old rotary-dial phone from inside the rock house.

My stomach dropped and I was sick inside just as I had been a few times before in my life at tragic events like the goat massacre—when death was in the air. Grief consumed me. Mr. York and his wife had been such an important part of my story-book childhood on the farm. Vivid images of red velvet cake—Mrs. York's specialty—those dreaded pig castration adventures, hanging tobacco in those rickety sheds, and those heavenly pony rides across the farm and up Nathan Smith Road to the York's rock house flashed through my mind. During the summer pony rides to see the York's with my siblings and cousins, honey suckle had always lined the Nathan Smith Road in the fence rows all the way to their house. The sweet smell of the honey suckle permeated the air at this moment as Bill and I continued along Nathan Smith Road toward the rock house.

As I entered through the front porch screen door, I saw Mr. York lying lifeless on the floor between the kitchen and the hallway. Sunlight coming through the back kitchen window shone like a spotlight upon Mr. York with a heavenly hue outlining his body. The soles of his brown, lace-up, ankle-high leather boots were facing me as I approached him. Mr. York was still, pale grey in color, and at peace. It was obvious that Mr. York's soul was gone.

A double-barreled twelve-gauge shot gun lay between his legs and flat on his chest. A self-inflicted fatal wound from the shotgun was visible in the center of his chest, outlined by crimson-red blood on his khaki shirt. The shotgun blast had propelled Mr. York backwards into his final resting position on the floor.

Another man from the greatest generation was gone. Like all those that I was fortunate enough to farm with growing up, I learned a tremendous amount from Mr. Douglas York, both while he was living and at his death. Life is so precious. I'm not sure if Mr. York ever owned any property. He leased the farm from the Smiths all those years that I knew him, but he took care of the land like it was his own.

I learned from Mr. York that we are really only custodians of the land while we are here on this earth. It's our responsibility to be good stewards of the land so as to pass it on to the next generations. After all, we are only a heartbeat away from passing from this side of the veil to the other.

The farm has exposed me to both life and death, helping me to appreciate life and gain a better understanding of the stark reality of death. There is a time to live, a time to die, and a time for everything under heaven. How glorious is it to see a lamb, a calf, a foal, or a goat kid born—but tragic, bad things like Mr. York's death are going to happen too.

We are all going to die someday, whether human or beast, unless we are taken up during the rapture. What we do with our time here on earth is up to us. Make it count. Some people prefer living in the city and that's okay. But for me, give me the farm life where I can be surrounded by the farm, animals, people, and the green pastures that I love.

Chapter Ten

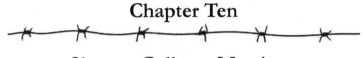

Sharon, College, Marriage

During the midterm of my senior year at the new Page High School, I caught the sight of a very cute petite girl carrying a bundle of papers as she walked past me down the hall. There was something about this girl that made me take a second look. She had big seventies' dark-brown hair, nice jeans, and a certain charm about her. It might not have been love at first sight, but it certainly was enough to pique my interest.

I found out from friends that she worked at the school office between periods delivering documents. Her name was Sharon. She wasn't a really a farm girl at all. Sharon and her family lived outside of Nolensville on a few acres of land, but she had no real exposure to a working farm. Most everyone called her "Mouse," presumably because she was small, cute, and quiet as a church mouse.

Sharon and I started dating. Our relationship grew as we dated during the school year, culminating in us going to the senior prom together. In the weeks that followed, I began exposing her to the farm and the rest of the Hatcher family. The farm and the Hatchers started to change Sharon, and Sharon embraced it. Change was necessary if she had any chance at all of being accepted by my family. Sharon was too timid, too light of an eater, and too soft-spoken to be any match for the outspoken, heavy-eating, and loud Hatchers. The change in Sharon was first noted at the dinner table. If she had any hopes of getting anything to eat at dinner or to communicate with the Hatchers, she had to be much more aggressive in eating and much louder when she spoke. She began to do just that.

Eventually, Sharon learned to get what she wanted to eat as the serving plates were passed the first time because there was no second chance. If she hesitated at all, she got nothing to eat: the eight or ten ravenous Hatchers sitting around the table like vultures made sure of that. My dad may have been the worst offender of eating more than his fair share. I can remember him asking as he was shoveling the remaining food on a serving plate onto his plate, "Anybody want any more?" Sharon learned to talk so loud during a conversation that even a Hatcher could not talk over her.

The total transformation of Sharon took some time; but by the second year of exposure to the farm and the Hatchers, the once terribly shy, soft-spoken, sweet little Sharon was never seen again. She became just as loud and as aggressive an eater as the rest of us. Sharon didn't have to accept the farm or the Hatchers or all the madness that came with it, but to her credit, she did. How many girls would give up the city life for the farm life, allow themselves to be changed so dramatically, and live amongst the crazy Hatchers? After all, farm life is not easy in itself; Granddad would be the first to tell you that. I think Sharon's transformation was a testament to how much she loved me and continues to love me, and I love her back for it.

I had known I wanted to become a veterinarian since the third grade in elementary school. After graduating from high school, my plan was to attend the University of Tennessee (UT) in Knoxville, in preparation for Veterinary School. I started college in the fall of 1976. My parents dropped me off in front of Hess Hall, my new home at UT. Hess Hall was called the "Zoo"

because of the nightly ritual of the inhabitants making animal noises into the center courtyard.

I had not preregistered by mail. In those days, there was no computer registration. The class registration lines were a half-mile long to sign up for certain classes. My roommate was a hometown boy named Jimmy Burton from Culleloka. He and I had wine and cheese parties, and cigar and poker parties, in our dorm room. We became lifelong friends.

The drive to Knoxville, Tennessee, from the farm without traffic was around three hours. I attended the University of Tennessee in Knoxville my freshman and sophomore years. Even though I would try to come home every four to six weeks, I missed Sharon and the farm a lot.

It's not that I didn't enjoy college life. My college years were some of the best of my life—with basketball, football, cheerleaders, and good cold beer by the pitcher, what's not to like? But this wasn't home; this wasn't the farm. I would write weekly letters to Sharon and my parents letting them know of my classroom struggles with chemistry and physics and how much I missed them and the farm. I always wanted to know what was going on there. How were the cows, had it rained, and had the hay been cut? I'm the eternal optimist and usually not easily depressed, but those two years were difficult for me. When I did come home to the farm and Sharon for the weekend, that three-hour drive afterwards back to Knoxville and arriving at my empty dorm room in Hess Hall was dismal.

Finally I couldn't take being away from Sharon and the farm any longer. I left Knoxville at the end of the spring quarter and returned to the farm. In the late summer of 1978 between my sophomore and junior year of college, Sharon and I were married in the front room of the home place—Lucy's house—in the presence of a small gathering of close friends and family. This was another spur-of-the-moment wedding, a precedent set by my granddad when he abruptly got married on the streets of Nashville in a horse and buggy many years before. Hanging on the wall of the room that Sharon and I got married in was a large black-and-white framed photo of my great-grandfather—Abram Wooldridge Holder—taken nearly a century earlier. The penetrating eyes of my great-grandfather in the photo seemed to intently watch the ceremony. I got the feeling that he approved of the union. My immediate plans for living arrangements were for Sharon and me to stay with my parents at the home place.

Since we couldn't live with my parents long term, it was my idea to go up and look at the old tenant house on the hill near the everlasting spring as a possible dwelling for Sharon and me. It had been abandoned for years. The old tenant house was a small house comprised of four small rooms including the bathroom. A double rock fireplace was in the center of the house. A cute porch spanned the width of the front of the house. The entire roof was tin. The house had been built from all poplar wood cut from the farm.

A beautiful maple tree at least a hundred years old anchored the southeast corner of the front yard, providing shade during all those years for my great-grandfather, grandfather, my father, and now me. There was one big problem, though. The house was extremely dilapidated and for several winter seasons had been the birthing area for the goats. Certainly these were not suitable living quarters for a beautiful new bride, but I was hopeful.

Sharon and I walked up on the hill to take a look at the goat-barn-once-house. Much to my surprise, Sharon was open to the idea of the goat barn as living quarters. We attempted to gain entry through one of the double front doors. Goat manure about six inches deep had accumulated in the house over the multiple birthing seasons, blocking the door from opening. I pushed against the door, using my shoulder with all my might, and opened the door just enough for Sharon and me to gain entry. It was a good thing we were both slender because the opening was only about a foot or so. For the first time, Sharon seemed to have her doubts about the whole thing. I tried to be optimistic and blurted out, "Maybe it will look better once it's cleaned out!"

Before clean up and remodeling the house on the hill. Sharon and I are standing in the doorway.

The next day, Sharon and I returned to the goat barn on a mission. We donned gloves to protect our hands as we shoveled the dried goat manure out the broken windows into the yard. The discarded goat manure piled up to the level of the windows outside the house. Beautiful poplar wooden floors discovered under the goat manure gave us reason to continue.

My future brother-in-law, Chubby, always the comedian, kicked the front door in, entered, and exclaimed while chuckling; "I can't believe you guys are going to live here!" From that point on, I was determined to make it work. The goats had to find new winter shelter.

A new urgency helped drive the project as Sharon was pregnant and due in late spring. Now we needed a nursery, too. My dad, my in-laws, and Sharon's grandfather supplied some money for the remodeling: kitchen cabinets, septic tank, water installation, furniture, and appliances. The house was completely gutted. We kept the double front doors but replaced the center rock fireplace with a double brick fireplace. The house remained four rooms. The nursery would be either in our bedroom or the living room. A waterline had to be run about six hundred feet across the big field to the everlasting spring, exactly where Granddad and his wife camped out in a tent some forty years earlier.

The fellow that put in the water lines, installed the septic tank, and dug the field lines in the side yard said that the topsoil on the hill was the deepest and most fertile he had ever seen in his life. I guess that was the reason my forefathers grew alfalfa hay, corn, and tobacco on the top of this hill.

While the back hoe was readily available, we had two concrete stock gaps placed in the ground along the long driveway coming up the hill for the purpose of cattle control. One was at the bottom of the hill and the other mid-way to our house. These stock gaps prevented us from having to open and close two gates every time we went up and down the driveway. The cattle were able to graze along the long driveway, keeping the fence rows cleaned out, but the downside was that our vehicle tires were always coated with fresh green cow manure. There is no way to keep your car clean if you live way up a gravel drive in the country anyway. It's a constant battle fighting accumulated dust, mud, and cow manure on your vehicles, even the car you take to town.

**If you look closely, you can see me
doing a handstand on the porch.**

We lived so far off the main road that Sharon and I used to joke that anyone coming up the driveway was either there to visit us or do us harm. Our little house on the hill on the farm was a slice of paradise. I had the freedom to chase Sharon around the house naked with no fear of anyone seeing me. We had no neighbors for miles. Life was good.

After clean-up and remodeling; note the top of Sharon's 1977 Camaro. Mr. Tomlin and I did the yard fencing.

We hadn't been living in the house long when one night the whole front corner of the house started vibrating down to the foundation, accompanied by a high pitched noise that hurt our ears. Sharon and I had no idea what was going on. Was it aliens? Was it an earthquake? I leaped from the bed, grabbed the twenty-two rifle Sharon's grandfather had given me, and bolted through the front door onto the porch in nothing but my underwear. I hollered out, "Show yourself or I'll shoot." I could hear a chorus of laughter coming from just around the corner of the house.

Emerging from the darkness was my crazy brother-in-law, Bill, and my mischievous, soon-to-be other brother-in-law, Chubby—my sister Lucy's boyfriend. They had decided to give Sharon and me a little house-warming gift, and this was it. The dirty deed was accomplished by attaching a waxed string to the corner of the house with a nail, drawing the string tight at a safe distance from the house, and then strumming the string for the desired effect—a very effective trick indeed.

The following year, Sharon gave birth to our first child, Jennifer. Sharon and I both were twenty years of age. We were practically kids ourselves and now we had a kid. *Now what?*

Jennifer coming home from the hospital.

When Jennifer was a few weeks old and had just become strong enough to roll over, she rolled off the diaper changing table onto the floor. Jennifer began to cry one of those cries where there is a moment of silence between cries so that she could catch her breath. This scared Sharon so badly that she began to cry also. With Jennifer in the car seat—both still crying—Sharon drove the car to the hay field where I was working because she thought that Jennifer might be hurt. As I drew closer to Jennifer to examine her, she abruptly stopped crying and flashed me a smile. That's when I knew everything was going to be all right.

That wasn't the only time while we lived in the little house on the hill that Jennifer was in harm's way. As it turns out, toddlers and brick fireplaces don't mix. In fact, we made two trips to the emergency room to get Jennifer stitched up for the same injury because of the brick fireplaces.

We had the same attending emergency room doctor each of our two visits to the hospital. I think he wondered what kind of parents Sharon and I were. Jennifer was first learning to walk when she stumbled and hit her forehead on the corner of the brick fireplace splitting her right eyebrow. There is something incredibly unnerving for young parents about bright red blood dripping down their child's cheek. Jennifer had just gotten out the first set of stitches when the exact same thing happened again, only the cut was a half inch higher on the same eyebrow. Today Jennifer has two barely perceptible scars on her right eyebrow.

Even though I had married, moved back home, and had a family, I continued forward with the distant dream of becoming a veterinarian. I was farming full time now with my dad, my brother George, and brother-in-law Bill.

Mr. Pagel and his family had moved away to manage another dairy on the other side of Franklin, so we were managing the dairy ourselves. I was attending Middle Tennessee State University some thirty miles away to obtain most of my required classes for veterinary school. My situation dictated that I take chemistry, organic chemistry, and biochemistry at the University of Tennessee, Nashville, and at David Lipscomb College in Nashville at nights and during the summers.

I struggled to adequately balance farm work with school work. Fortunately, my grades were good in everything but organic chemistry and biochemistry. They were my most difficult classes. Much to my displeasure, I got a D in biochemistry, damaging my chances of getting accepted in to veterinary school. I applied to veterinary school three times: the first time as a junior, the second time as a senior, and the third time after graduating from Middle Tennessee State University in 1980. Each time, I received a letter stating, "We regret to inform you that you have not been accepted into this class. Please try again."

My graduation from Middle Tennessee State University in 1980; note band aid in Jennifer's eyebrow.

On a beautiful, sunny, late-summer day in 1981, I was stacking alfalfa hay on a wagon in the big field behind our little house, near the same spot my grandparents had camped out years earlier, when Sharon hollered at me off the back porch while waving frantically. She shouted, "It's the Vet school on the phone and they want to know if you would accept a position in the incoming class as an alternate?"

I responded loudly across the fields. "Are you kidding me? Yes, yes!" as my heart leaped for joy.

Jennifer helping me *study* chemistry.

I had been working toward this goal for years. I had mixed emotions though because I knew I would have to leave the farm again. Sharon, Jennifer, and I had grown accustomed to living in the little house on the hill and we liked it. Moving to the city would be very difficult for all of us. For now, I had a few months to prepare for our departure and enjoy my last days on the farm. I didn't realize it then, but we would not return to the farm for thirteen years. Even though I had wanted to become a veterinarian since I was a kid, one of the hardest things I have ever had to do in my life was to move away from the farm. It was a necessary step, though, to accomplish my dream. As I look back on it now, it was God's plan and it was good. My life would have been much different if I hadn't become a veterinarian.

Sharon's parents helped Sharon and me load all our earthly possessions onto a poor man's moving van, a twenty-foot cattle trailer—after washing the cow manure out. We headed for East Tennessee towards the veterinary college. My days of having no neighbors for miles in any direction were over.

As we entered Knoxville on Interstate 40, I pointed out the married student housing to Sharon on our right as we took the wide sweeping exit toward the Smoky Mountains. Married student housing was a ten-story, drab, red-brick, worn-out looking building. The realization that we had moved from the near perfect life on the farm, living in the little house on the hill, to something like this must have hit Sharon at exactly that moment. She wept as she exclaimed, "I'm not living in a cracker box!"

**Headed to graduation at Middle Tennessee State;
see old yellow *Toyota* 4-wheel drive truck.**

Tears of anguish rolled down her cheeks. Young Jennifer, around two years old at the time, sensed there was something wrong with her mother and also burst into tears, adding some vocalization for effect. Here I was with two women in the vehicle crying as a direct result of my goal of becoming a veterinarian. What a fine mess I was in.

I started veterinary school later that fall in 1981, placing either last in my class or next to the last; I never knew which one for sure. There was at least one other alternate in my class.

Sharon and Jennifer both made many sacrifices during those years in vet school. Sharon took a full-time teller job at the local bank just to make ends meet. Little Jennifer was either in day care or at the veterinary college if the day care was closed. She was practically raised at the vet school in her early years. It wasn't uncommon for Jennifer to be spotted in the arms of the professors in the halls between classes or toddling along with the live-in students whose responsibility it was to receive emergencies after hours. All was a foreshadowing of what Jennifer would become: one of the finest veterinarians in the country.

Our first place to live was a one-bedroom duplex apartment out Alcoa Highway, about eight or ten miles from the vet school. The apartment was all we could afford, and the commute to the vet school wasn't too long. School was foreign to me since I had been farming for almost a year and a half since my graduation from Middle Tennessee State University. I soon realized that the sheer volume of material one was required to digest at vet school required me to stay current in my studies.

My usual daily routine was to go into the bedroom, shut the door, sit down at a small desk, and study three or four hours. My rule was not to stay up past midnight, unless of course Sharon and I were disco dancing. After all, this was the eighties.

The areas of study that were hardest for me were neuroanatomy and pharmacokinetics. I was fortunate enough to have the Dean's daughter as my anatomy and study partner for the first year. If it hadn't been for her, I don't think I would have made it through. I believe I made two C's that first year. As I settled in and we started to actually handle live animals, I caught stride. I could solve real-life problems better than I could learn from a book. I had started at the bottom of the class, but in the end, I was toward the top.

After we had spent nearly a year in the apartment, I was missing the farm. Homesickness gnawed at me from the inside. I had heard from the locals that a dairy farm in Maryville might need some help. I went out to the farm to take a closer look.

Sure enough, they did need some help. I struck a deal with the owner. I would take care of the baby calves and do some light farm work in exchange for a place to live on the farm rent-free.

We affectionately called the house we lived in the "Green House" because it had this dreadful green siding on it. The house was not well insulated and there were cracks in the outside walls. The living conditions reminded me of the home place where I grew up, hot in the summer and cold in the winter.

The red-wasp-alert bed check was reinstituted in the summer months just as when I was a kid. My study area was off the back of the main portion of the house on a concrete floor in a small room that was really nothing more than a closed-in small back porch. It was as cold as ice in there during the winter. If it was snowing and the wind was blowing just right, occasionally snowflakes would float through the walls and land on my desk only to melt and disappear. Sharon and Jennifer never complained. We had each other. We were living on a farm again and that made everything all right.

I made a lifelong dear friend while living on that dairy farm. His name was Steve Cornett. One day as I was feeding the baby calves milk outside the dairy barn, I heard a good rendition of *Little Brick Houses* by John Cougar coming from inside the dairy barn in a pure, perfectly in-tune, falsetto voice. Listening closer, I heard yet another song, *More Than a Feeling* by Boston. The high pitched voice singing along with the radio struggled to hit the high notes on this one, but still managed them.

I walked inside the milk barn to see who this obviously happy person was. It was Steve singing along to the radio while he was milking cows. Steve and I became fast friends. We had common interests. We both loved milk cows. Steve is undoubtedly the best "cow man" I know. Better than anyone, he understands how cows think and feel and what it takes to get maximum milk production. I have never known anyone that enjoys dairy farming as much as Steve. I was so impressed with Steve that I asked him if he would help manage our dairy back home. He agreed and managed our dairy for several years before moving on to a better opportunity. Steve has been in the dairy business ever since, and he is still my friend.

After a year and a half of vet school, there was a party for my class to celebrate our half-way point to graduation. I got a little bit carried away at the party. I began to drink champagne out of the bottle and by the bottle on the dance floor as the night progressed. I don't remember how much champagne I consumed or much more about that night. However, I remember the next day vividly. The next morning I arose around 7:00 a.m. so that I could go to the vet school and SOAP my hospital cases. SOAP stands for subjective, objective, assessment, and plan. It was mandated that the vet students had to perform SOAPs on all our hospital cases over the weekend.

On route to the bathroom I became nauseous, so I lay down in the middle of the kitchen floor. Sharon obviously had no sympathy for my current state and, hoping to teach me a lesson for my indiscretions, ran the vacuum cleaner around my head as I lay on the floor. I did eventually get up knowing I needed to complete my SOAPs at vet school or face the consequences. Since that day, I have never been able to drink champagne. Sharon's vacuum therapy must have worked.

In the early spring of 1984, I did an externship with the man who I thought was the premier dairy practitioner at the time, Dr. Jenks Britt of Russellville, Kentucky. The veterinary practice was in south central Kentucky in a prime agricultural area that was rich in row crops, dairy, and beef and swine operations. I got along well with everyone in the practice. It was a perfect fit for me as far as a veterinary practice goes. The externship went so well that Dr. Britt said that the practice would offer me a job upon graduation. I liked the possibility of doing dairy practice there. Graduation from veterinary college came in June of 1984.

At graduation, I received an award in proficiency in food-animal medicine. I was no longer at the bottom of the class. The offer from Dr. Britt didn't come through after graduation, so I fell back on a job offer I received from a mixed animal practice in Manchester, Tennessee. I had worked at the veterinary practice in Manchester for about eight months when one night the house phone rang; Dr Britt was on the other end of the line. He said they were in a position now to offer me a job and wondered if I was interested. I didn't have to think twice—yes, I was interested. This was my chance to learn from the best and to be the best veterinarian I could be. This wasn't home, but I didn't feel like I was ready to start my own practice where I grew up, at least yet. Sharon, Jennifer, and I were making another move, this time to Kentucky.

Graduation from Veterinary College in 1984.

Chapter Eleven

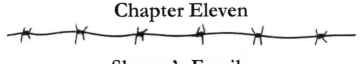

Sharon's Family

Sharon's grandparents were George and Lucille Johnson. We called them Granddaddy and "Boo." Jennifer named Lucille "Boo" because when Jennifer was a toddler Lucille always said "Boo" to her. Boo was the original stay-at-home mom. She waited on Granddaddy hand and foot. I never saw her dressed in anything but nice flower-print dresses with stockings rolled down to knee level, very prim and proper.

Granddaddy was a self-made man, a stranger to none, and he loved to talk. He left school early, ending his formal education after the sixth grade to make a living for his mother by delivering milk in glass bottles by horse and buggy. His father had passed away when he was six, just as my grandfather's father had. It must have been common in those days for young men to become gainfully employed at an early age to help support their families.

Granddaddy was a people person who had a knack for business. He became a real estate agent, developing a successful real estate company called Johnson Realty. Sharon's father, William—"Red" or "Parker," as I call him—was partners with Granddaddy in the family business. Their office was in a trailer park in Nolensville, Tennessee, which they also owned. Granddaddy was a man of his word and a firm handshake was his bond. That's the way he did business—a rarity in today's world.

Granddaddy Johnson taught me two very important life lessons. He always used to tell me, "Boy, take anything someone will give you" and "Never get so bent out of shape with someone you can't do business with them because someday you may need to." I translate that as *take anything that is free* and *don't burn any bridges.*

**Sharon's grandparents and father,
Sharon holding newborn Jennifer.**

Granddaddy and Boo had two children, both boys, named William and Paul. William, Sharon's father, was the oldest. There never have been any two kids that were more different. Polar opposites, William was cautious while Paul threw caution to the wind. William didn't like to gamble or take chances; Paul did. William was conservative with money; Paul was not. William was a Democrat, Paul was a Republican. Paul enjoyed life to its fullest, often having a good time. If William had a good time, he wouldn't admit it. And so on and on the differences went.

Paul, being somewhat of a rebel, chose not to enter the family real estate business but instead go out on his own. No surprise there. Risk-taking was more Paul's cup of tea; real estate development was his game. The business risks didn't bother him at all. He developed several projects that hit really big, putting him in a very strong financial position for the rest of his life.

At the age of twenty-nine, William was diagnosed with a slow-progressing form of Multiple Sclerosis. Everyone, including William, thought William would succumb to Multiple Sclerosis and be the first to die of the family. But he didn't. Granddaddy died first of heart problems, then Boo, then Paul in 2004 after a long, courageous fight with cancer.

I am not a religious fanatic, but I always wanted God to speak directly to me. At one time, he did, though not where I expected him to do it. It was at Paul's funeral in 2004. I can honestly say that I thought people who said that God had spoken to them were crazy until it happened to me.

The funeral was more of a celebration of life. The selection of music set the tone. Paul loved Elvis, so there were several upbeat Elvis tunes. Willie Nelson sang as only he could *Blue Skies from Now On*. The preacher gave a short message describing Paul to perfection: giving, upbeat, positive, and fun loving. The immediate family and I moved to a smaller more private room where the casket was open for a final viewing of the body. That was where it happened.

After a few minutes of silence with us gathered there at the front of the casket, Paul's business partner stepped to the side of the casket to say a few words. I suspected that he might be Jewish, as he wore a small black cap on the top of his head. He began to chant rhythmically in an unrecognizable language, presumably in Hebrew, enunciating words deep from inside him with such inflection and passion that spit was spraying intermittently from his mouth.

Here's the totally amazing thing: I began to recognize every word. It was Psalm 23. When he came to the verse, "and he causes me to lie down in green pastures," I was completely engulfed by the presence of something communicating a message to me. There wasn't an audible voice that I heard, but the message was clear, calming and unmistakable. God said, "I am the God of the Israelites and I am your God, too." Okay, go ahead and add me to the list of crazy people that say God has spoken to them. I'm just relating what really happened to me.

After that day, Psalm 23 become my favorite scripture, especially the part about green pastures, galvanizing my faith, consoling me, and helping me during difficult times. I can relate to green pastures not only because of this experience but also because of the importance of green pastures in our farming operation and in my life. The days when the farm has lush green pastures are the cows' and my most content days. I like nothing more than to sit or lie down in our green pastures amongst the clover, watching the cows happily graze and listening to them pull grass. A sense of peace and of refuge always comes over me, protecting me from anything this world can dish out.

**Practicing veterinary medicine
as a young veterinarian.**

Chapter Twelve

Kentucky Vet to Tennessee Dairyman

In 1985, Sharon, Jennifer, and I moved to Russellville, Kentucky, where agriculture is king. Agriculture is by far the number one industry and also the way of life there. I had a diverse bunch of dairy and beef clients ranging from traditional farmers to the more conservative black car and truck-driving Mennonites, to horse-and-buggy Mennonites, to the most conservative draft-horse Amish. One thing in common about all of them was that they made their living farming, just like what I was used to growing up. They were the salt of the earth.

Things at the family farm were changing again. My friend, Steve, who I had met while in vet school and who was managing the family dairy, had moved on for a better opportunity in east Tennessee. My brother-in-law, Bill, took a job at the *Nissan* plant in Smyrna, near Nashville. Nobody was left to milk the cows. In October of 1985, our parents sold the dairy cows and heifers at auction on the farm under a tent. It was a complete dispersal.

Since I was in Kentucky actively practicing veterinary medicine, I was helpless to do anything about the change. To me, the auction was like a death in the family and left the same empty feeling deep inside. The dairy barn now stood empty as a constant reminder of what once was, like a kind of museum. The wooden stanchions were dust-and-cobweb-covered with a few feed buckets scattered about as evidence that cows were once milked there.

Now that the milk cows were gone, I had to find a good

use for the farm land. I struck a deal with our good neighbor Mr. Robert White to run beef cows on the farm. His cattle of choice were Brahma. He liked them because they were resistant to heat and pinkeye, but they were known to be very high-strung when you worked them.

Robert could do more with less than anyone I ever knew, and he always made money. The simple, low-cost cattle-working facility he built nearly thirty years ago is still being used today. It doesn't look like much but works surprisingly well. I learned all my electric fencing skills from Robert White. Unlike Mr. Tomlin's fences that took time to build, were costly, and were constructed to be permanent, Mr. White's electric fences were made quickly, inexpensively, and meant to do the job right then. I learned from Robert that a little is all you need, only enough to get the job done—anything above that is a waste. One can get by with what one has and make it work. Have a plan and just do it; no sense whining about how little one might have.

I only ever saw Robert in three different work outfits. The standard outfit was faded blue jeans; brown belt; a sweat-stained, long-sleeve khaki shirt; lace-up, ankle-high, brown-red wing boots; and a worn straw hat with a built-in green visor on the front. I also saw him one time in almost the same attire, but changed up a little by his using bright red suspenders instead of a belt to hold his pants up and a ball cap instead of the straw hat. In later years, when his health declined, Robert, in order to be more comfortable, wore blue farmer's coveralls instead of the blue jeans, but he still wore the same khaki, long-sleeve, sweat-stained shirt.

Robert kept one of those pocket-sized spiral note pads in his bib pocket with all his cattle records on it. No need for a smart phone or electronic device for record keeping—they weren't invented yet, anyhow. Robert White and I had a very good business and personal relationship. The farm made enough money from the beef cow operation during the years Robert White managed the farm to pay the land taxes.

I thought my years in Kentucky would be few, just enough to be trained and then return home. A few years turned into a decade more of being away from the family farm. The veterinary business thrived in Kentucky and at its peak had three veterinary practices. I honed my skills as a dairy practitioner. I began to travel some and had scheduled dairy herd visits in both Tennessee and Kentucky.

The veterinarian was the top of the social ladder, even above the medical doctor in Russellville, Kentucky, because of the importance of agriculture in the area. Little Jennifer loved riding in the truck with me on farm calls in the evenings and on weekends. Her training as a veterinarian started as soon as she could walk, while I was in vet school, and continued while we lived in Kentucky.

Sharon became pregnant with our second child while we were in Kentucky. She gave birth to our son, Charles, on January 2, 1987. Charles was the first baby born in Logan County, Kentucky in 1987. I can remember thinking that my life on this earth was now complete since I had a son to carry on the Hatcher name. If I died now, it would be okay.

My father Abe came to Kentucky and stayed with us for that first week after we brought Charles home from the hospital. Dad was much more of a caregiver than my mother. He came to Kentucky many times to visit while we lived there. Both Jennifer and Charles have fond memories of Dad cooking for them and playing with them.

Life was good in Kentucky. Despite this, the pull back to the farm that I loved so much was powerful. I began to think about reopening the dairy operation. My little brother, Jim, six foot two-and-a-half inches tall and eleven years younger than I, showed some interest in reopening the dairy as well. We talked about it; both agreed, and we formed a partnership called

RockNRoll Farms. A few years earlier, Dad had given Sharon and me one hundred and eighty-four acres of the over five-hundred-acre family farm. The dairy barn was on the portion of the farm that Dad had given to us.

Jim didn't realize it at the time, but he was going to make caring for the farm his life's work. I am eternally grateful to him for that; had he not, there would have been no continuation of the family dairy or Hatcher Family Dairy as we know it today.

Jim cleaned up the old stanchion flat barn, which is a level concreted area with wooden head catches to secure the cows' heads while being milked. He poured some concrete, made other improvements, and brought the facility up to Grade A dairy standards. The dairy had been resurrected. We were issued a Grade A permit in the fall of 1992. Jim was twenty-three years old. The dairy was back. We bought about thirty Holstein cows from a dairyman in Eagleville, Tennessee, and started milking them.

Weekend trips back to the farm from Kentucky became more and more frequent after the dairy opened. We would either stay with my parents, Sharon's parents, or my sister Lucy. Fearing we might wear our welcome out, I met with a good friend of ours we knew from church, Riley Sewell, about the possible construction of a weekend cabin. There was an old blacksmith shop and an old corn crib, both made out of logs, within sixty yards of the milk barn. The shop and corn crib were badly in need of repair. I wanted to preserve these log structures and everything they represented. Just think of all the eared corn that had been stored in the corn crib or how many horse shoes had been forged in the blacksmith's shop!

Instead of repairing the old log structures, Riley and I decided—with Sharon's blessing—to use the pre-Civil War poplar logs from the two buildings to construct a modest log cabin at the same location. The beautiful logs were at least a foot wide and deep. We numbered them, disassembled them, and then reassembled them on a prepared foundation at the same site on which the corn crib once stood. The weekend cabin was small, basically consisting of one big room and two lofts with ladders on each end. The very tiny kitchen with trailer-home-sized appliances and the bathroom were beneath one loft, and the living/dining area was beneath the other loft. The cabin was just the right size to meet our immediate weekend needs.

The frequent trips home to the farm made me realize that it was time to return to the farm for good. Riley and crew were asked to come again to add a front porch, mud room, master bedroom, and master bathroom. Since we had used all the old logs that were available on the farm, we acquired similar old poplar logs from a neighbor to complete the expansion.

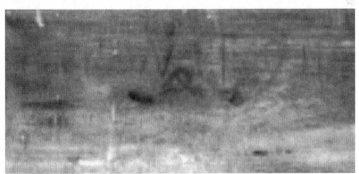

Barely visible in the photo are the initials CWH carved by my namesake, my granddad's brother, Charles Wooldridge Hatcher in 1894. I carved my initials below his in 1973.

The historic poplar board piece with the initials CWH carved twice on it was placed over my back door porch frame in 1994, one hundred years after the original Charles Wooldridge Hatcher had left his mark. The inscriptions there today are a constant reminder to me of my Hatcher heritage on this farm every time I look up and see them as I enter the back porch door. I wouldn't be here if it weren't for those who came before me and the work that they did. I don't want to ever forget that.

I began to make preparations in Kentucky for our move back home to the farm. Dr. Kevin Vance, my business partner, and I owned two veterinary clinics at the time: Logan County Animal Clinic in Russellville and Todd Logan Veterinary Services in Guthrie. Kevin had the same aspirations as I and wanted to move back home also. We were able to sell Logan County Animal Clinic rather quickly to one of our associate veterinarians, Dr. Jon Todd. Jon had married a Logan County girl, so it was a logical fit for him the buy the clinic. We were not as fortunate in selling the Guthrie Vet clinic.

I turned my attention to building a veterinary clinic on the farm. Some of my Mennonite carpenter friends came down from Kentucky and built a very nice pole barn, fifty-five feet by one hundred feet, as a veterinary facility. For two years, I traveled back and forth between the two clinics until the Kentucky clinic was finally sold. I surely must have needed my head examined, but sometimes you just have to do what you have to do. We opened the Tennessee clinic in the fall of 1993. A friend of mine told me we should name the vet clinic RockNCountry since the farm was RockNRoll, and so we did.

The dairy was doing fairly well by that point. The vet clinic was open and starting to do some business. It was time to move home. I wanted to spend more time with my family, especially my parents as they advanced in age. We sold our house in Kentucky and moved home in time for Christmas 1993. For this move, we rented a *U-Haul* truck instead of using the stock trailer. It was a wonderful Christmas indeed that year.

1994 storm

In February of 1994, an ice storm of epic proportions descended upon most of Tennessee and southern Kentucky. The electric lines and tree branches were no match for the heavy covering of black ice, and they snapped like banjo strings, causing power outages for hundreds of thousands of people.

Power outages are a major inconvenience for the general public but a downright disaster for livestock operators, especially dairy farms. Even though you can milk a cow by hand, try milking sixty cows twice a day without machines. It's impossible. Before the ice storm hit, Sharon and I had gone back up to Kentucky to finalize our business affairs and had left the kids on the farm. We were stranded in Kentucky with no way to get back to the farm. Our kids, Jennifer and Charles, ages fifteen and seven, stayed with my parents and my sister Lucy on the farm. While staying with my parents, Jennifer and Charles slept in a twin bed by the wood stove.

My brother Jim had his hands full trying to get the cows milked. He assembled every able-bodied person with good hands to milk the cows. That included everyone who lived on the farm: my kids, my parents, and all my brothers and sister and their kids. Those present fought over the cows with long teats because these cows were easier to grip and milk. There was one cow in particular called Martian that had the longest teats. She was the favorite of all to hand milk.

In the end, the family was only able to give the cows some relief on their udders once a day. By the third day, Jim had borrowed a tractor-powered generator capable of barely running the milking system. The milk, however, had to be dumped since the milk truck couldn't get in to pick the milk up. In all, the power was off for five days.

My kids walked over hill and dale to my parents across the farm on a regular basis for food and warmth. Dad kept the wood stove going and made them hot *Ovaltine* drinks, roasted almonds, and toasted bread with sharp cheddar cheese on the fire. My sister Lucy fed them as well, and they had great fun making donuts in the home place kitchen. The ice storm for them was a great adventure.

Meanwhile, Sharon and I were in Kentucky, helpless to assist on the farm at all and not having nearly as much fun. Most things recover with time, and it was no different after the ice storm. Some were without power for weeks, but eventually things were back to normal. The dairy had survived another setback.

Father's death: February 17, 1994

I was still traveling back and forth between the Tennessee and Kentucky vet clinics because I hadn't sold the vet clinic in Guthrie yet. I stayed many weekday nights in Kentucky at my receptionist and her husband's house. They were generous hosts.

Not long after the ice storm, I was in Kentucky one fateful morning on a dairy herd health visit just south of Russellville when I got word my father had had a major heart attack at home. He had been transported to Williamson Medical Center, and was not doing well at all. That same sick feeling deep within that I had felt at the goat massacre when I was a boy and when I first saw Mr. York lying dead on the floor at the rock house came back. I immediately dismissed myself from the herd visit and sped off in my *Jeep Cherokee* vet mobile.

I remember traveling at a high rate of speed through Nashville on Interstate 65, sometimes reaching speeds over one hundred miles per hour with my emergency flashers on. There was this sort of numbness that crept over me as I drove to the hospital. Memories of Dad flashed in my mind, his crazy, bright-colored sunglasses; his high-riding pants; that sweet, sweet smile; his generosity toward everyone, including complete strangers; and his innate ability to calm me even when a problem seemed too big. Something told me that Dad had passed. Calmness ensued, presumably from Dad's fleeting spirit as he passed, one last gift from him as he left this earth.

As I exited Interstate 65 South onto the Franklin exit, miraculously the three traffic lights turned green in synchrony, giving me free passage. When I arrived at the hospital and entered the emergency room, there was no activity, just stillness. I asked the nurse about Abe Hatcher. She confirmed that Dad had passed away.

I had moved back to the farm only three months before Dad's death. I have always regretted not moving back sooner so that I could have spent more time with Dad. The nurse directed me up the hall, then pointed to a door and said, "He's in there." I went through the door. There on a stainless steel table lay Dad's body, lifeless, grey, and cold just as Douglas York's body had appeared to me years before. It was obvious to me that Dad's spirit was gone. This was just a corpse now.

Dad had donated all his organs to those that needed them, just as he had given everything else away his whole life. There was an immediate need for his corneas. They were scheduled to take his eyes as soon as all the immediate family had viewed the body.

I didn't know until Dad died that he wanted to be cremated. It was a bit of an unusual scene at the funeral home for those coming by to pay their respects. Many were visibly uncomfortable when they entered the funeral parlor to realize there was no casket or body in the back of the room as was customary in the south. There were photos displayed around the room of Dad enjoying life and smiling, as he often did.

I have always felt since then that this was more of a celebration of Dad's life than mourning, although at the time, his sudden death was a painful shock. Looking back on it now, I think a quick death is much preferable to a slow, suffering death or living with Alzheimer's for a long period, as we are experiencing with my mother presently.

Dad's memorial service was held in the historic Presbyterian Church in downtown Franklin, Tennessee, right off the square. All seats were full, with standing room only. Everyone knew who Abe Hatcher was, how giving he was, and how he lived his life. Dad was a servant all his life. People there shed tears of sorrow and joy that day while listening to the preacher tell real-life stories—some very funny—about Dad.

Later that week, on a clear, cool, brisk, early spring day, Mom and all the kids and the two dogs ascended Robinson Hill to the southern face. All of us took turns spreading Dad's ashes in the wind, dispersing them back on the farm Dad loved so much. From that day forward, Robinson Hill was called Abe's Mountain.

I believe Dad's death strengthened both Jim's and my own resolve to continue farming the land that had been in the family since 1831, now for five generations. The best chance we had of passing the farm on to successive generations was to continue dairying. We knew it was tough, though; Granddad had made that abundantly clear before his death. The nature of the dairy business is to struggle and to have some financially good years sprinkled amidst a long line of bad years, and so it was with us. This was going to be a whole new frontier without Dad as our anchor.

Chapter Thirteen

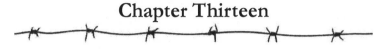

Animals We Have Loved

Two dogs

Animals have always been important to me, which is why I became a veterinarian. Farm animals have given me a whole new appreciation for God's creatures. An old man told me one time that if you are fortunate, you will have one really good dog in your lifetime. I have had two. The first really good dog I had was a half-German shepherd, half-Australian cattle dog named Abe. I named the dog after my father.

Jennifer, Charles, myself holding Abe, Sharon.

Abe was red in color and looked like a red heeler but a little taller because of the German shepherd influence. As intelligent dogs tend to do, Abe looked me right in the eye anytime we communicated with each other. I could see it in his deep brown eyes: he forever wanted to please me, always awaiting my instructions when in my presence. Abe was a working dog; riding in the back of the vet truck, he made every farm call I made.

Abe saved my life—or at least saved me from bodily harm—twice. The first time, I had just performed a breeding soundness exam on a very large Brangus bull. Apparently the bull was not happy about the procedure and abruptly charged me with deadly intent after I let him out of the chute. I was backed into a corner and had nowhere to run. Just as I prepared for the crushing impact of the angry bull, Abe vaulted himself toward the bull, latching his pearly white teeth onto the bull's nose as he came between the bull and me. The bull stopped his charge, shaking his head violently to remove Abe. Abe released his grip. The bull retreated, much subdued, loading himself onto the awaiting cattle trailer. The bull was ready to go home.

The second time Abe saved my life happened in downtown Nashville after dark. As I was leaving the Fairgrounds from a sick cow call in the bad part of town, two questionable characters approached the truck shouting obscenities with unknown intent. Abe lit up like the Fourth of July, barking, lunging, and gnashing his teeth in their direction. They fled.

Abe was very protective of me and my truck. He was meaner than a junkyard dog to everyone but me and my daughter Jennifer. Abe didn't even like my wife Sharon. He would often softly growl at her. Abe acted very differently towards me, though. He dislocated his hip one time jumping out of the truck. A dislocated hip is one of the most painful conditions a person or animal can have, but when I told him to lie still on the exam table while I treated him, he never once offered to bite me.

Abe was so smart that he knew Sunday was church day.

You may doubt me, but he did. If I exited the house in the morning with work clothes/coveralls on, he would jump into the back of the vet truck because he knew it was time to go to work. If I came out of the house dressed nicely, he wouldn't even raise up from his sleeping position because he knew I didn't need his services.

Abe also saved me many steps when getting the cows up to be milked. I could direct him to the far end of a field where the dairy cows might be and he would bring them down to the barn to be milked. He loved nipping their heels if they didn't move to suit him.

Abe's reputation as being a good cattle dog spread far and wide. Many wanted to use him as a stud dog and some did. All his puppies were extremely intelligent and changed the lives of all who received one.

I lost my faithful companion one fateful day on a farm call in Leiper's Fork, Tennessee. I had driven to a beef farm to pregnancy-check some cows. That day, I had a veterinary intern riding in the truck with me, and we were engaged in conversation all the way to the farm call. When we arrived at the farm, I noticed that Abe was gone. He was not in the back of the truck. I looked for Abe the rest of that day and the next day and the next day but found nothing. I offered a reward, posted lost dog signs at the country stores, and desperately looked for him in the following weeks to no avail—there was not a trace. Abe was gone. I never really got over it.

Years later, the second great dog came into my life by total surprise. On my birthday in 2010, to my great amazement my kids presented me with an adorable registered red Australian cattle dog puppy. They had driven seven hours, almost to the Tennessee/North Carolina border, to get him. This ten-week-old pup was the cutest little energetic, playful pup you ever saw. I struggled with what to name him when I arrived at simply "B," like B in the alphabet. This dog is a complete opposite to

Abe in many ways. He likes everybody and Abe really only liked me. B also has no cattle skills, whereas Abe was skillful at cattle herding.

Jennifer with B.

B was the first Australian cattle dog I have known like him; he was actually sweet. B's sole ambition in life is to play, have as much fun as possible, and be with me. His idea of fun is to run, on a whim, in circles at full speed through puddles of water, over and over again.

B has a whole basketful of toys in our living room. When I come home in the evenings, he greets me with excitement, wanting to play fetch or chase with me with each and every toy in the basket. Whether it's been five minutes or five days, he is always happy to see me. B and I chase each other around the house making circles through the kitchen and living room until Sharon demands that we quit. B truly enjoys life as much as any creature I have ever known. He is the only one I know that appreciates the farm more than I.

B looks at me with his deep, orange-brown, penetrating eyes, reflecting nothing but unconditional love and affection that makes any day better. We take walks or run through the pasture lots, including where Granddad camped in the big field and down to the everlasting spring. B loves to chase red squirrels, wild turkeys, and rabbits. Just like a person, B rides in the cab of the truck, sitting erect in the passenger seat and intently watching out the window, taking it all in as we travel down the road.

Tug-of-war with a heavy rope and playing fetch with a ball or *Frisbee*—or practically anything—are his favorite games. His vertical leap when he jumps to fetch something is about four feet, which would land him first place in the NFL combine.

B has no fear. I don't think he is scared of anything if I am with him. Going up a flight of stairs, a ladder, or off an embankment are all no problem for him, especially if I go first. B would follow me anywhere, no questions asked. B sleeps in a kennel at night in the house office. In the mornings, when I let him out of the kennel, instead of heading outside to relieve his bladder, B comes to me first to say good morning and check in like he hasn't seen me in a long time. He won't go outside until I tell him it's okay to do so. I have had two once-in-a-lifetime dogs—how fortunate am I! B truly is one of my best friends. I don't know what I would do without him.

Cows

Our cows are like members of the family. Some of these cows are particularly special to us; they have been selected by the Hatcher Family to be in the Hatcher Cow Hall of Fame. Similar to other Hall of Fames, entry into the Hall is based on a lifetime body of work. There are currently five cows in the Hatcher Cow

Hall of Fame, all deceased. They are Brownie, Suckalala, 1500, Emma, and Jevon. All of them lived to a ripe old age, and all of them are buried on the farm. Each cow provided a lifetime of service to Hatcher Family Dairy by producing milk and impacting our lives in a special way for many years.

Brownie was a Brown Swiss cow with excellent body conformation, correct feet and legs, and a beautiful udder. She transferred in from another dairy because she could not adapt to a large, confinement-type dairy operation. This would be comparable to saying that my preference is to live in the country because there are some things about living in the city that I can't tolerate.

Brownie was a massive but gentle cow—gentle enough that one could walk up to her in the field and place a halter on her. Brownie milked six lactations—six years—after coming to our farm. She is responsible for all four of the Brown Swiss cows we have on the farm today. Giving all the way until the end, Brownie delivered twin heifers weeks before her death as a very old cow. In her honor, Brownie was immortalized on every label of our world famous chocolate milk, which bears her name: "Brownie's best."

My brother Jim and son Charles with Brownie.

Old 1500 had no name. She was another transfer that couldn't adapt to a large-confinement dairy operation. 1500 was an older cow when she arrived on the farm. There was nothing pretty about her. She had bad feet and legs, and her udder confirmation wasn't good either. But she was a blue-collar worker that came to work every day, month after month, year after year, until her death.

Putting in at least eight years of service at Hatcher Family Dairy, 1500 was the grand old lady of the farm. She was the oldest working cow I have ever had the pleasure of having as an acquaintance. We never really knew how old she was, but 1500 was at least sixteen years of age upon her death. No one had a better work ethic.

Actually, there was something pretty about her: she had the most beautiful bold-white blaze on her head and matching white gleaming teeth that made for the most wonderful smile you ever saw. She is pictured smiling on the side of both of our delivery trucks. 1500 was photographed while grazing—working—in wheat and red clover in the big field near the everlasting spring. She was a testament to how one can love one's work.

Suckalala was a small Holstein cow with a big heart and a will to milk. My kids named her as a calf because she would not suck the milk bottle aggressively. They called this lack of aggressiveness, "suckalala-ing" around, thus "suckalala." The name took. She was the kids' favorite from the start. Pound for pound, she was probably the most productive milk cow we have ever had. Unfortunately, she was three-titted. One of her quarters was blind and produced no milk at all, but she still managed to consistently produce over one hundred pounds of milk per day.

More like a dog than a cow, La-La responded when one called her name. If she was within ear-shot, she would look up and come to you. She was so tame that Charles would ride her off the hill when getting the cows up. La-La had a modeling career as well, managing to be in at least two advertising campaigns as a cover girl. When La-La passed away, everyone on the farm mourned for a month. She had a heart as big as Texas.

Some of our good friends and fellow dairy farmers brought a darling, registered Jersey heifer calf to us one day in a dog kennel as a gift. She might have weighed forty pounds soaking wet. Our friends wanted my kids to show her in 4H dairy cattle shows. The Jersey calf was named Emma. Emma grew up to be a majestic Jersey cow and represented her breed well by winning many dairy shows. With an infectious personality, Emma won the hearts of many people. She came across with a genuine sense of friendliness and caring, although at times she refused to be led by a halter, balking when she didn't want to go.

Emma was always the star of all the parades Hatcher Family Dairy participated in, elegantly promenading through the streets of Leiper's Fork, Franklin, and College Grove. Emma seemed to enjoy all the attention that she got.

Emma in the center at the College Grove Christmas parade. Also pictured, left to right: Tucker, Jim's old Golden Retriever, Brother Jim, and Sister Lucy, wife Sharon, myself, and niece Jessica.

Lastly, Jevon, named after Jevon Kearse of the Tennessee Titans during his rookie season, was our last inductee into the Hatcher Cow Hall of Fame. By mistake, I had given her a boy's name, not realizing she was a female until after I had tagged her. Rather than cut the tag out and rename her, we decided to just stay with the name Jevon. She is the most beautiful and elegant of all the Hall of Fame cows—the prototype of what a dairy cow should be, the ideal cow, and Charles's favorite. Jevon milked at least ten consecutive lactations—she looked good doing it, too—until retiring after the birth of twins at the age of thirteen. We decided to permanently turn her out to pasture to allow her to raise her twins until the end of her days.

It was not a good day when Charles found Jevon down and unable to stand in her retirement lot. Charles called Jennifer to come and examine her. It was apparent that Jevon was not going to get up. Her advanced age coupled with a failing liver required that she be put down.

Jevon's death had a profound effect on Charles. I didn't realize he thought so much of her until this occurred, but I should have known. The two of them had grown up together on the farm. Charles, when eleven years old, had raised Jevon from a baby on a bottle, then later milked her twice a day for at least a dozen years. Upon her death, Jevon was nearly sixteen, and Charles was twenty-five. I have seen no human-animal bond stronger than the one Charles and Jevon had.

Charles insisted on burying Jevon alone. He buried her near the massive oak tree at the lower edge of what we call the granary lot. He dug the hole with the front end loader attached to the old blue *9600 Ford* tractor. Charles dug the hole deep, gently placed Jevon in the grave, and then lovingly covered her with dark rich dirt. The burial took all afternoon. It was a time for Charles to say goodbye to Jevon in his own way. That's the way he wanted it.

Chickens

I never knew that chickens had personalities until Sharon started into the free range egg business a few years ago. I always thought chickens didn't have enough sense to get out of the rain, but that's not the case.

Sharon calls the hens her ladies. At feeding time, the hens respond to Sharon's voice and circle her in great anticipation of receiving a little chicken feed to supplement their grass and insect diet. A few of them come up to her feet to crouch down to the ground with the expectations that Sharon will pet them like a dog. Sharon's favorite chicken is Henrietta. She is always the first in line seeking Sharon's affection.

The hens are rotated onto fresh pasture on a regular basis, although they are contained by moveable electric netting that surrounds a hen house on wheels in the center. Inevitably, the same two hens breach the electric netting during the day to adventure around the calf barn, searching for tasty insects and worms of all types. In a regular nightly ritual, as the sun starts to set, the same two hens come back to the hen compound. Standing outside the netting, they wait for Sharon to raise up the electric netting so that they can scurry under, returning to the safety of the compound.

The electric netting has a dual purpose. It keeps the hens—most of them—in the designated pasture lot as well as keeping predators out. Sharon has a dreadful fear that her ladies could be massacred at night by a menacing mink or weasel because this actually happened to some friends of ours. The hens go to bed in the hen house soon after dark every night. The last thing that Sharon does before she goes to bed is to close the door on the hen house as an added safety measure for her ladies. Predators would have to breach the electric netting and the walls of the hen house to reach her precious hens.

People at the farmer's market say eggs from Sharon's ladies have the most orange yolks and are the best eggs at the market.

Chapter Fourteen

Farm as Haven

As the years passed by, William—Sharon's father, my father-in-law Parker, and called Red by his friends (he has many affectionate names)—gradually became more affected by the Multiple Sclerosis. It crippled him to such a point that he became confined to a wheelchair or motorized cart.

In 2001, several years before his own death, Paul built his brother William a totally handicap-accessible, beautiful one-level brick house in his last development project subdivision. He specially built this house for William, I think, because he loved his brother so much and wanted to take care of him.

Gabaga and Parker lived in this house happily for many years until about 2008, when Parker became so weak in his legs that he began to occasionally fall. Sometimes he would fall when Gabaga was out grocery shopping or running errands. Since he did not have either the strength or necessary amount of control over his lower extremities to get up, Parker would have to lie where he fell until Gabaga returned. The frequency of the falls increased, and after a few more years passed, Gabaga was unable to get Parker up by herself.

We all lived some forty minutes away from Gabaga and Parker. When Gabaga called one of us for assistance in helping Parker up, it was a two-to-three-hour ordeal that included the drive over there, helping Parker up, and then the return trip. Parker was emotional after a fall and often in tears. I know he felt helpless about the falls, knowing there was little he could do to help himself.

Sharon had about reached her breaking point. She told her father that in his current condition, we would be better suited to help him if he and Gabaga lived closer to us. Sharon recommended that they try to find a house in the College Grove area near the farm. Parker, already known for being stubborn—stubborn as a mule, in fact—immediately resisted, becoming almost belligerent about the issue.

Months passed. Parker's falls continued, finally building to an emotional crescendo between Sharon and her father. Something had to be done. Sharon issued an ultimatum to her father, of whom I was supportive: either he bought a house close to the farm, built a house on the farm, or moved into assisted living. Much to my surprise, within days, Parker chose to build a house on the farm. He chose to build the house in a spot nestled between the lovely old oak trees that towered at the bottom of the hill behind the milk store and the veterinary clinic.

Parker is the type that doesn't like change. He is set in his ways and once he makes his mind up, there is absolutely no way to change it. Parker was hell-bent on building a house identical to the one that Paul had built for him ten years prior. The only changes were a slightly larger kitchen, a slightly larger two-car garage, and a brick fireplace. He reminds Sharon and me frequently that he built the house for us, especially the fireplace. After all, he says, "I'm not going to be around much longer." It's ironic to me when he says that because he has already outlived the rest of the family and may very well outlive us as well.

Construction began in the house in January of 2011 and progressed rapidly to completion. Gabaga and Parker moved in August of the same year. None of us ever really thought that Parker would move to the farm, and now it was a reality. We had a party in celebration. I know that Gabaga and Parker's move to the farm from Nashville was absolutely the best thing for them to have done, although Parker may never publicly admit it.

All Parker's life he had been an avid hunter/fisherman with a great appreciation for nature, wildlife, and animals in general. In his twilight years, he is now surrounded by red squirrels, wild turkeys, rabbits, birds, deer, and the dry cow lot—the maternity pasture where all the dairy calves are born. He takes great delight in watching the calves being born and feeding the wildlife in his back yard.

Bags of birdseed and corn are kept in his garage. Feeding the wildlife is a daily ritual. The wild turkeys are so accustomed to Parker feeding them that they have become like yard chickens. I happened to look up toward his house one day and saw a tom strutting in all his glory on the very clean, magnificently sealed, and shiny aggregate concrete driveway just outside the garage door. To his credit, the beautiful and colorful broad span of feathers and protruding chest were working for the tom. He had successfully attracted an interested group of hens for a love fest, which ensued a short time later outside Gabaga and Parker's garage door. I called up to Parker's house and told Gabaga what was occurring right outside their house and to witness the turkey carnage themselves.

Parker loves the daily interactions with the wildlife and farm animals. The farm has become a refuge for him. Despite his frail and declining physical state, his mind and spirit have become stronger since moving to the farm. The verses so eloquently chanted in Hebrew at Paul's funeral from Psalm 23—fearing nothing even when walking through the shadow of death—are being acted out here on the farm between Parker and his Maker.

Consummate playboy

My brother Jim was for much of his adult life the consummate playboy. Jim is tall, blonde, and handsome with a boyish grin. Women were and are instantly attracted to him. He has the same sharp jaw line and long legs as my father.

For most of Jim's life, there was a revolving door of gorgeous women in his life, from *Hooters* girls to airline stewardesses, until he reached the ripe old age of forty. When women got too close to Jim, he would perform evasive maneuvers to escape and continue his elusive search for the perfect woman. Just when we thought Jim would be a bachelor all his life, he met Jorie. She was a stunning brunette who possessed the wit and disposition necessary to deal with Jim's smug, often moody temperament.

The most eligible bachelor in Tennessee was married on November 13, 2010. Jim always wanted a son, but out of the union came a beautiful little baby girl. Her name is Hattie Lee Hatcher. I think God gave Jim such a precious little girl to change his life. Jim has a tender heart like my father and would give you the shirt off his back if he thought you needed it. But he guards his heart carefully, I think to keep from getting hurt. It's hard to get hurt if you don't let anyone close. Underneath Jim's crusty protective covering, there is a vulnerable soft gooey tenderness.

Hattie has ripped that cover off, exposing the goodness and making Jim's heart accessible. Hattie's demeanor is much like her mother's: cheerful, easy going, and always smiling. Nevertheless, it is hard for me to believe that Jim sired a child so sweet. The only explanation is that Jorie and Hattie are gifts to Jim directly from God, making life on the farm that much better for all of us. I'm thankful for that.

Most people say that Jim couldn't have a son that looked any more like him than my son, Charles. From a distance, it's hard to distinguish between the two—same body type, same facial features, and same mannerisms, including the wild flailing of the arms that many Hatchers are prone to.

Jim and Charles work together now, both of them playing critical roles at Hatcher Family Dairy.

Chapter Fifteen

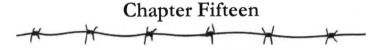

Troubles and Survival

Corner house—Beth

My sister Beth married Bill Wallace in 1974, and was the first of the Hatcher siblings to get married. The old former toll house sitting on the corner of Arno and Nathan Smith Road was empty. It was the logical place for Beth and Bill to live. However, it was in a bad state of repair. Bill, along with his father Marvin and Marvin's best friend, Rainey McCall, went to work on the old house, repairing the floors, windows, roof, and siding.

Marvin was a character. Everyone knew his signature look: a ball cap slightly cocked to one side and covering a full head of hair. Marvin was a sailor during World War II. He was always in a good mood. In some ways, Marvin reminded me of *Popeye the Sailor Man*—happy, loud, and always fun to be around. The remodeling of the house took several months. Marvin and crew did a fine job getting the old toll road house ready for Beth and Bill.

Bill and Beth lived in Granddad's log cabin until moving into the newly remodeled house in 1975. The house was tiny, with five small rooms: kitchen, living room, bedroom, bathroom, and an upstairs attic bedroom. As the years passed, both their boys, John and Willy, were raised in the little house, sleeping together in the upstairs bedroom.

An *Ashley Warm Morning* wood stove was installed in the living room to heat the house. A large pile of split wood was kept to the left of the house a short distance from the front porch. In the winter time, that wonderful scent of a fresh fire burning spread outdoors into the cold air around the house.

The only water source for them was a shallow well that produced an abundance of pungent sulfur water so strong the water was slightly black. The sulfur water stained all it came in contact, including the sinks and the commode. It smelt like rotten eggs and reminded me of the sulfur water at my grandparents on my mother's side years earlier. It's not uncommon for some wells to have sulfur water, and some people even say there are health benefits associated with it, but I never did care for it.

Beth and Bill and their boys lived in the meager little toll house for nearly two decades. Their dream was to one day build a new house on the farm. Bill was part of the dairy operation until the family sold out in 1985. When the cows were sold, Bill went to town and got a job as a mechanic but eventually gained employment at the *Nissan* plant in Smyrna.

On Easter morning of 1995, it became clear that something was terribly wrong with Beth. She hadn't been feeling well for about a week, although she continued to work. I stopped by to see her at the old toll house. She was extremely pale and anemic. I was shocked at how sick she was. Bill took her to the local hospital, and the doctors there immediately transported her to a Nashville hospital. Something had reduced Beth's red blood cells to a critical level. Either she wasn't producing red blood cells or something was destroying them or both. If this were a dog or cat, my most likely veterinary diagnosis would be leukemia, and that's what it was. Beth had acute myelocytic leukemia. She was so anemic that she required an immediate blood transfusion. The doctors called the family into the hospital because of Beth's critical condition; they weren't sure if Beth would live through the night.

Beth did survive the night. This was the first of three times that we thought Beth might die during her battle with cancer.

The next day the doctors broke the news to Bill about the severity of Beth's condition. Her only chance for long term survival was a bone marrow transplant, and even then the survival rate past five years was between ten and twenty percent.

The family was in shock. This was the first time that we had to deal with cancer with an immediate family member. All of us Hatcher siblings were blood tested to see if we were a suitable match for a bone marrow transplant for Beth. The only match out of the four of us was George. Intensive chemotherapy had to be used to fight Beth's cancer before the bone marrow transplant could take place. Since Beth was as weak as a kitten, the chemotherapy could not start for weeks until she became strong enough to withstand it.

Bill did the bulk of the sitting with Beth at the hospital, but to give him some relief, we developed a schedule for family members to sit with Beth. Everyone took a shift. Beth was not only weak, but her platelet count was near zero. Platelets are critical for blood to clot. Lucy, George, Jim, and I donated platelets to Beth for weeks. The platelets were collected from us in an over three-to-four-hour process by cycling blood from a catheter in one arm through a machine to remove the platelets and then back through another catheter into the other arm to return the blood back to our bodies.

Cancer can strip away every ounce of dignity a person possesses. Beth lay in the hospital bed with a hospital gown partially covering her frail, naked, pale body for weeks. She was so weak she could not raise her arms or go to the bathroom. Beth was totally dependent on others to survive.

The chemotherapy for Beth did start a few weeks later. Its purpose was to kill the cancer before it killed Beth. The doctors had to take Beth to the brink of death, destroying her leukemia-riddled bone marrow so that George's bone marrow could do the job. She became so ill that the family was called in a second time because Beth might die, but she didn't.

George withstood the painful procedure to harvest the bone marrow from his hip without complaint. The lifesaving bone marrow was given to Beth via an intravenous catheter. Beth's body rejected George's bone marrow, resulting in the third time we thought she might die. All told, Beth was in the hospital for close to a year.

In the years to follow, all the other patients that had been in Beth's cancer ward died except Beth. She was the sole survivor.

While Beth was in the hospital, Bill began construction on a brand new house for them that sat atop the hill on the eastern edge of the farm, overlooking the valley below. We knew Beth was scheduled to come home from the hospital, but the new house wasn't ready yet. So we applied a fresh coat of paint to the inside of the old toll house and did a deep cleaning in preparation for Beth's arrival back to the farm in the late fall of 1996.

A few months later, they moved into the new house. Their dream had come true. Sometime later, the old toll house on Nathan Smith Road was bulldozed down and burnt along with the rock house where Douglas York and his wife had lived in order to clear space for Interstate 840. The structures may be gone, but the precious memories that I have of that stretch of Nathan Smith Road remain.

After Beth returned to the farm, her leukemia went into remission and has remained in remission to this day. Her brave fight against cancer was successful, but the leukemia has left her crippled, making it difficult for her to walk and leaving her in constant pain as the transplanted bone marrow continues to do battle with her body. The fact that she survived at all is nothing short of a miracle.

Since her recovery, Beth has made it her life's mission to

provide support for other cancer patients as well as anyone who is sick. She knows what it is like to be helpless and as a consequence knows the importance of helping others who can't help themselves.

George

Since 2009, I have been Tennessee State Veterinarian. Every state has one. It's the state veterinarian's job to protect the health of the animals of their respective state. My office is on the south side of Nashville at the site of a plantation that was acquired by the state after the Great Depression. The campus is called Ellington Agriculture Center. The campus is a beautiful place to work, with plank fences, large oak trees, gorgeous flowers, and old horse barns on the property.

I received a text when I was at work at my office one afternoon in 2011 that simply read, "Brother George has had a major heart attack and he is at Williamson Medical Center, Lucy." Almost immediately, my last experience at the same hospital, when Dad was there, entered my mind; the end result had not been good. I jumped into my car and sped away toward the hospital. I couldn't help but wonder—would the outcome be the same, would George be dead when I got there, like Dad?

George and I were close while growing up. Once, when he was sixteen and I was fourteen, we made an adventurous camping road trip to Florida in the family hatchback *Subaru*. What possessed our parents to approve our trip I do not know. For two early teenagers to travel without adults in today's world would be asking for trouble. On our first night in Georgia, the campground that we had selected to spend the night in the back of the *Subaru* turned us away, thinking that we were runaways. Undaunted, we continued down the road until we found a campground that would take us.

That night at the campground, George and I were invited to a party on the beach. Thinking we might get in trouble somehow for going to the party, we turned the invitation down. I could kick myself now for not going. But what a spectacular time we had on that trip, camping, fishing, and swimming in the ocean!

After entering adulthood, however, George and I drifted apart. Each of us married young, started families, and led separate lives. Driving to the hospital, I was overcome with emotion, realizing that I might not ever see him alive again or have an opportunity to improve our relationship.

When I arrived at the hospital, a small, stunned group had gathered in a waiting room at the end of a hall, consisting of Lucy, Diane—George's wife—Diane's parents, and George's preacher. The situation was grave. Apparently, that morning while George was vigorously working out, he was having a heart attack and didn't know it. Diane finally convinced him to go to the hospital to get checked out.

After they arrived at the hospital, while Diane was checking George into the emergency room, George proclaimed to the doctor that he felt better, and then promptly went into a complete cardiac arrest. The doctors attempted to resuscitate him for at least fifteen minutes after his heart stopped, shocking him eight times. George's heart was finally restarted but was not acting as an effective pump.

On this fateful day, providence dictated that a highly trained cardiologist happened to be at the hospital; he saved George's life by installing a balloon pump via catheter to assist George's ailing heart. George's condition was so grave that he needed to be transported by ambulance to the cardiac unit at Saint Thomas where they were better suited to treat him.

We all looked on as they rolled George by gurney down the long hallway toward us. There was total silence except for the rhythmic noise of the ventilator breathing for him and the balloon pump pumping blood to his lifeless body. A white sheet covered George except for his head as if he was already dead. That same aura of death surrounded George as was present in the end for Dad and Mr. York. George's face and lips were grey and appeared cold.

Diane kissed him tenderly on the forehead. We all knew the seriousness of George's condition without the doctor saying a word. The reality was that they didn't really know the extent of the heart or brain damage, whether he would survive or not, and if he did survive, what his mental status would be. As they rolled George's nearly lifeless body down the hall to be loaded into the awaiting ambulance, people on each side continued to work on him. I really thought this would be the last time I ever saw George on this side of eternity.

George was in a coma state for four days and on life support in a well-staffed intensive cardiac unit that was affectionately called "the pod." He had tubes literally coming out of every opening of his body, plus some extra holes that were made for more tubes to enter. The control panel for all the machinery looked like the captain's deck of the *Starship Enterprise*.

Many of us camped out at the hospital for those four days. The visits to see George were controlled and short. He was unresponsive during the visits in a coma-like state. On one of my visits in to see George, an apocalyptic revelation appeared to me. Looking at George in that hospital bed, I saw in my mind's eye the Hatcher generations flash before me. I could see myself, my brother Jim, my son Charles, my father Abe, my grandfather George, and my great-grandfather. Abram Wooldridge Hatcher, all at one point in time. *What did it all mean?* Was it a reminder of the importance of the generations, of my ancestors who had worked so hard to keep the farm before me? Or was it a wakeup call that we are all a heartbeat away from meeting our Maker? I'm thinking maybe both.

The family has always known that Lucy's daughter, Jessica, has a special connection with the Lord God Almighty. When she prays to him, she says, "God, it's me," as if God knows her directly. I'm sure He does. Jessica prayed over George when he was in that delicate place between life and death, separated only by a thin veil. She held George's hand and prayed out loud, slowly, simply, and deliberately, in the way that only Jessica can.

George did wake up from that coma early in the morning on the fifth day. Much to the pleasure and surprise of the medical professionals, George had no permanent heart or brain damage. He would make a full recovery in the months to follow. Several years before his heart attack, George had already made the change to a healthier life-style of diet and exercise. The cardiologist said besides the intervention of the Great Physician—God—one reason for George's recovery was that he was physically fit.

The left descending coronary artery of George's heart—dubbed the widow maker—was totally blocked, causing the massive heart attack. George's experience prompted me to have a CT scan done on myself to determine the amount of calcium on my coronary arteries. Calcium is an indicator of plaque. The scan showed that my left descending coronary artery is affected with a mild amount of plaque, which has prompted me since George's heart attack to do four hours or more a week of vigorous cardiovascular exercise.

George had stories to tell of his death-to-life experience. Many people were interested in his stories, and George felt that he was called to relate his experiences to all who would listen. George said that during his coma state, he definitely felt a powerful healing surge flowing through his body when Jessica laid her hands upon him.

George also saw that light at the end of the tunnel referred to by many in near death experiences. He walked toward that light, entering into what he said was heaven. Bright colors present in a blue sky, green grass, and pure white sheep were intense, making George feel completely at peace where he was. His descriptions reminded me of the colorful mountain scenes of *The Sound of Music* when Julie Andrews was dancing around holding her hands up toward the heavens. A clear voice proclaimed to George in heaven, "Your work is not done; you need to go back." George walked back through the tunnel toward life, exiting out the other end of the tunnel back to earth. That's when he said he flew over and around the world like *Superman*. First, he flew over the farm and saw all of us as we waved to him one by one, and then he flew overseas, looking down on those in foreign countries that were praying for him. Immediately after that, he woke up and was back with us.

George's heavenly experience has changed him. His mission now is to finish the work he was commanded to do. As a result of his experience, all of us understand the fragility of life and my relationship with George is improved. We are brothers once more, now not only genetically but spiritually, too.

Origin of *Farm Strong*: YMCA wise counsel

I was already exercising on a regular basis before George's heart attack, but I began to exercise in earnest after realizing my family's history of heart disease. If my schedule permitted, part of my lunch hour was now spent at the local YMCA within a few miles of my workplace. I became fast friends with three or four others around my age and older who also frequented the YMCA during lunch hour. This core group of men became my life advisors. I often seek their wise counsel during difficult times or if I have questions about business today. When we are together, it is mostly fun and games at the gym, but a healthy competition does exist between us during our workout sessions. Each of us has certain exercises that we are best in, and we all take great satisfaction in beating the others in these exercises. The person that does the most repetitions of a certain exercise or handles the most weight is the winner and has the bragging rights that go with it.

Although I am the smallest of the group, I excel in certain upper-body strength exercises. One day, after I completed the most reps for a shoulder/arm exercise competition of the group, one of the counsel said, "Hatcher, you are *Farm Strong!*" What he said that day resonated in my head. This was the beginning of *Farm Strong* and the title of this book. To me, *Farm Strong* means much more than the physical strength acquired by living and working on a farm. It means being mentally and spiritually strong, too.

Mom

Some years after Dad's death, Mom moved into the quaint little cottage right behind the cabin that Mom and Dad lived in for so many years off of Nathan Smith Road, on the north side of the farm. The move allowed Jim to occupy the cabin and to begin a family. Mom was in her late seventies.

Jim's living so close to Mom enabled him to conveniently check on her as she advanced in age. During this time, Jim (and the rest of us, too) began to notice some early signs of memory loss in Mom. These were little things at first, like forgetting where she parked her car, but they advanced over a year or two to the point that she would become disoriented when driving to town and unable to find her way.

Eventually, after her doctor's diagnosis of dementia, we took Mom's *Volkswagen Jetta* away from her out of safety concerns for her and others. Taking Mom's car away from her was very difficult for us. She never understood why her car was taken away and insisted that she was a good driver.

In an answer to prayers, Mom decided on her own to move to an assisted living facility in Tullahoma, Tennessee, to be with her sister, my Aunt Trish. Aunt Trish had never married and was a retired school teacher. She had been stricken with polio at an early age, which caused some serious health problems all her life, and was now in a wheelchair.

Mom moved into a corner room right across the hall from Aunt Trish. At first, Mom didn't seem to like her new setting. Soon, though, the tenants of the facility learned of Mom's prowess in tickling the ivories at the piano. Mom likes nothing better than playing the piano for others. Music is one of the few things that dementia has not stolen away from her. She can still play Beethoven as well as anyone.

Aunt Trish's condition worsened, requiring a higher level of care than she was receiving at assisted living. She was transferred to an advanced care unit in the same town. With Mom's sister in a different facility, we made the decision to move Mom back closer to the farm so that we could visit her more regularly. Mom is presently in the memory care unit of an assisted living facility owned by the same company as the assisted living facility in Tullahoma, which is very close to my work. My frequency of visiting Mom has greatly increased. I try to go by and see her two times a week.

Watching Mom go through this advancing, worsening dementia and losing her most precious memories—especially those of my father—has been one of the most painful experiences of my life. However, I receive great joy in going to see Mom, even though she may not be able to call my name or know whether I am her son or brother. In certain good ways, Mom acts like a child now. She recognizes me instantly when I walk through the door and shrieks in delight. She tells me she loves me every few minutes when I'm in her presence, and there is nothing better than that.

Chapter Sixteen

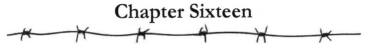

Progress and Its Costs

Interstate 840

Around 1985, rumors of an interstate highway possibly going through southern Williamson County and by-passing Nashville were circulating in the countryside. Dad in the late seventies had portioned out the farm to all of us kids. The rumors soon became reality as state government officials started coming around. As it turned out, the route for Interstate 840 was slated to go right through Beth and Bill's portion, effectively dissecting the farm in half.

The northern half where Mom and Dad and Jim lived on Nathan Smith Road would become isolated from the rest of the farm, thus requiring a massive bridge to be built over Interstate 840 to give us access to our own land. The coming of Interstate 840 was another sign of the decline of agriculture in our area.

Construction began in 1991, taking around seventy acres of our farm and devouring countless other family farms. The heavy equipment, bulldozers, trucks, and earth movers loudly roared, nauseously echoing through the hills for days, weeks, and months. The constant chattering of steel, wheels, and engines was haunting.

The productive creek bottom hay fields where I had spent many hours making hay and parts of the creek where I had caught minnows as a kid were forever gone. This was progress accomplished by the painful sacrifice of precious, productive farm land. The farm witnessed the current devastation and mourned. It had seen a lot of things over the years but nothing like this. The very fabric of the farm was penetrated like a gunshot through the heart by the interstate construction. We could only hope that Interstate 840 would not be a mortal wound.

Overlooking the farm on the hill before Interstate 840. Abe's Mountain in the distance.

More progress

In the fall of 2007, an eleven-hundred-acre development project right across the road from the farm gained final approval by the Williamson County Planning Commission. The project, called Laurel Cove, swallowed up five neighbor farms directly across Arno Road from us. It was a one hundred twenty-one million dollar project. Planned was an eighteen-hole, pro-style *Greg Norman* golf course; fitness center; coffee shop; over eight hundred half-million to million-dollar-plus homes; and all the accompanying amenities.

Similar to the Interstate 840 construction, heavy equipment rumbled for over a year. During that time, the dust and noise were constant. Piles of dirt appeared like mountains against the horizon. Sometimes the heavy equipment started before daylight and continued into the night. The clattering of heavy equipment could be heard as the cows were gathered to be milked.

Dust is a part of life on a farm with gravel roads during the dry months, but the construction across the road took dust to a whole new level. Every vehicle we had, tractors, cars, and trucks alike, was covered with a quarter-inch layer of dust. Whenever I went to town in one of our vehicles, I was a little embarrassed. My poor little red *S15 Chevrolet* truck was filthy compared to the pristine, high-dollar automobiles of the city dwellers. The layer of dust on the windshield of my truck had to be rinsed off with the barn hose so that I could see through the windshield before I went to town.

Arno Road for a half-mile stretch or more had to be widened to accommodate all the anticipated new traffic. As Arno Road was widened, the vet clinic and the milk store were shut off from main traffic for eight months; our places of business were as isolated from civilization as if they were on a deserted island. Finally, the Arno Road widening was complete. What a drastic change from the way things used to be. I have a picture taken over twenty-five years ago of my father holding the hand of one of my nephews as a toddler while they walked down the center of Arno Road in broad daylight. Today, there is a steady stream of traffic on Arno that intensifies greatly in the early morning and late afternoon when commuters are going and coming from work and school. Walking down the center of Arno Road now, whether day or night, would mean almost certain death.

The golf course was almost complete and they were selling lots for house construction in Laurel Cove like hot cakes when the recession hit. The project was financed entirely by *Lehman Brothers*. When they went bankrupt, everything came to a screeching halt. The workers and sales team left. I occasionally saw a security person guarding what supplies remained, but I think he finally left, too.

Heavy rains washed topsoil over the already completed roads within Laurel Cove. The large piles of dirt remained untouched, stacks of pipes and construction material lay undisturbed, weeds grew uncontrolled, and heavy construction equipment was scattered around, seemingly abandoned right where they were after their last use. Laurel Cove looked like a ghost town.

The irony of it all was that Hatcher Family Dairy survived the recession, but Laurel Cove did not. To me, Laurel Cove represented all the money in the world or maybe greed itself, and it all collapsed. Although I was sad from the very start to see the development take beautiful productive farmland, it was my hope that the project would someday be completed. The new situation was a total waste.

Months and months went by with only rumors of the project starting back. We thought several times about turning the milk cows on the golf course to graze. Finally, after more than two years, an investment group with a history of salvaging failed projects bought Laurel Cove out of bankruptcy for ten cents on the dollar.

The project started anew. The name was changed to The Grove. The workers returned; a rebirth began. Gradually, we noticed improvement. The infrastructure was rebuilt and repaired, including the clubhouses, roads, and entrances. Trees were planted and a wooden fence was put up all along the perimeter of the development. Extensive landscaping with rock walls dressed every entrance. None of the rocks used for the walls were obtained locally, which stood in sharp contrast to my small rock project just across the road where the walls were built by the hands of the owners.

New houses seemingly sprouted up from the ground. I could count at least six houses under way at any one time. I was beginning to wonder how our new neighbors would react to a dairy farm being right across the road. What would they think when they get that first whiff of aromatic cow manure when we pumped the lagoon? Or what if a fly landed on their picnic dinner? Or one of our cows escaped the farm and began grazing on one of their well-manicured lawns? Time will tell whether we can coexist. We do plan to be good neighbors. We want to educate them about where their food comes from. Hopefully, they will become our customers and drink our milk; our sustainability and the future of Hatcher Family Dairy depend on it.

Chapter Seventeen

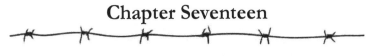

The Decision

Parlor barn

From the year 1992 until 2000, we milked the cows in a flat barn. That means that the cows and the people milking them were all on the same level, on a single, flat, concrete floor. This arrangement works well and one definitely has close contact with the cows, but it also leaves the person milking the cows vulnerable to a swift kick from cows that were prone to do so. The cows that kicked were called kickers.

The majority of the herd would never even lift a foot, but there were some that had a bad reputation for kicking. One of the worst kicking cows we ever had was an Ayrshire cow we affectionately called Whippett. Whippett would rapidly whip from side to side while simultaneously kicking with intent to cause harm to the person brave enough to attempt to apply the milking unit to her.

We used a couple of techniques when applying the milking units to kicking cows: the shoulder technique and the head technique. The objective of both was to apply steady but firm pressure with your head or shoulder against the cow's side just in front of the udder to keep the cow from kicking as the milking unit was applied. I preferred the head technique because it protected my head by burying it in the cow's side. At least I wasn't going to be kicked in the head.

At the end of a milking, I had every color of cow hair from the kicking cows on my head, neck, face, and arms—really all over my body and clothing—mixed with fresh cow manure, all of which formed a nice, concrete-like, colorful coating. If I lost the battle with Whippett, I would also be battered and bruised or limping because, at some point, I would have hit the concrete. If I was fortunate, when she kicked me, her back leg would lift me up and toss me out into the center alley out of harm's way. If I was unfortunate, she would kick me under the neighbor cow to be thoroughly trampled.

For safety reasons and to make it much easier on the back of the milker, my brother Jim decided to remodel the barn. The change would broaden the pool of those willing to milk, since milkers would no longer have to fear the kicking cows' threat to life and limb. Jim is very mechanically minded and took the remodeling project on himself. He did most all the work himself with help from his friends.

The plan was to convert the flat barn to a parlor barn. This type of barn has two levels. The cows are on one level and the milkers—people—are on a lower level below them. This puts the milkers out of harm's way and also prevents them from bending over when applying the milking units. To do this remodeling, Jim needed to dig a pit in the flat barn for the lower level. All the milking cows were moved for eight weeks to a dairy in East Tennessee where my friend Steve Cornett was the managing partner.

We purchased a used, double-eight, parallel stanchion from a dairy down the road that had gone out of business. A stanchion is a wood or metal framework which restrains the cow while being milked. Jim broke out the concrete of the middle section of the old flat barn in order to dig a pit about ten feet deep, twelve feet wide, and twenty feet long. We cut the double-eight stanchion down to a double six and installed them on each side of the pit. A set of stainless-steel butt plates, complete with troughs to catch the cow's urine and manure, were also installed on each side. Jim poured all the concrete, including the drains for the wastewater, and he did a masterful job. Jim was very proud of the new double six parallel parlor barn. At the entrance of the milk barn, he inscribed into the concrete when it was still wet, "Jim 2000."

Our local dairy service man completed the remodeling of the milk barn by furnishing the parlor with new, stainless-steel, two-inch milking lines; wide, full-view *Delaval* milking claws; pulsators; and a larger milk pump.

After that, it was time to bring the cows back home. Because every other family member was busy working on the farm, Sharon and a dairyman neighbor of ours had the dreaded task of hauling the cows back from East Tennessee some two hundred miles away. Eight big, heavy cows to each trailer was the maximum load.

While coming down the dreaded steep decline of Monteagle Mountain on Interstate 24, Sharon had a blow-out on one of the trailer tires. Miraculously, she was able to maintain control of the truck and trailer, preventing what could have been a deadly event for her and the cows. Sharon confronted me when she finally arrived back at the farm, declaring that she would never haul milk cows again.

When the cows arrived late that afternoon, a marathon milking ensued. This was the first time any cows had ever been milked in the freshly remodeled milk barn. It was an exercise in futility. Each cow had to be individually pushed into the parallel stanchions by Jim, Charles, and me. Not until 10:00 p.m. did we leave the milk barn, exhausted, sweaty, and reeking of cow urine and manure, only to repeat the same thing the next morning.

We were beginning to have second thoughts about the whole remodeling project. However, each successive milking took less time. The cows soon accepted the change, actually liked it, and settled into the new parlor barn in time. We were glad the old flat barn was gone. Remodeling was a good idea after all.

The dairy business is much like a roller coaster. There have been high points and low points and thrills followed by disappointments. The RockNRoll farms—the partnership that Jim and I formed in 1992—has had a few good years financially, but most of them have been bad. The bad years were so difficult that more than once we considered folding the tent, wondering why we were working this hard for nothing.

Although we were building our assets in cattle and in equipment, many times we had to borrow money against our equity in order to pay bills. Jim and I were spinning our wheels and getting nowhere. All our milk was being sold to a Farmers Cooperative at a wholesale price. The milk was picked up by a large tanker truck and shipped south to one of several processing plants with which our Farmers Cooperative had contracts. A Farmers Cooperative is a group of dairy farmers that collectively markets the milk of the group. The Farmers Cooperative (Co-Op) does the best it can in marketing the milk for the group, but in the end, our Co-Op had no say over the price of the final product since they were really a wholesaler of the milk to a processor. The identity of our milk was lost. There was no way for us to add value to our milk.

A bottling system

In 2005, I attended a conference at Tennessee State University in Nashville. One of the speakers was a dairyman from South Carolina who had added value to his milk by bottling his own. He described how he had his own bottling facilities on his farm and how it had helped improve his finances tremendously. I was intrigued. A seed had been planted in my mind, and I couldn't stop it developing. I wanted to have the ability for us to determine the price of our milk, too.

I telephoned the dairyman in South Carolina, quizzing him on costs, benefits, and the trials and tribulations of being a producer/processor. Sharon and I drove into Alabama to visit another dairy that was adding value to their milk by processing. They had a drive-through on their farm for customers to buy their products. I was more convinced than ever that we needed to do something similar. I had several conversations over many months with my brother Jim about making the plunge, but he wasn't going for it.

I knew it would be a huge investment for us to bottle our own milk. It made sense to me that we should do our homework first and get some help before we jumped into the processing business. The Center of Profitable Agriculture, a non-profit group comprised of the Farm Bureau and Tennessee Agriculture Extension working together to help farmers, did a feasibility study and business plan for us. The report was not really encouraging.

Sharon and I sat down with our county extension agent, the fellow that had done the study, at the kitchen table to review their findings. We needed to bottle over ninety percent of our current milk production and sell it for six dollars a gallon to be able to service the incurred debt. The realistic chances of us doing that the first year were slim to none. I was devastated but not deterred.

Looking back on it, the study and business plan were right on the numbers. It wasn't easy, but we had all the necessary ingredients to succeed: dedicated key family members, location, and the ability to produce a quality product.

Middle Tennessee State University (MTSU), where I did my undergraduate studies, had a small, fluid-milk processing facility on campus about thirty miles away from the farm. I approached them about bottling some milk for us to test the market. The initial response was lukewarm. They said working within their current budget would be near impossible.

Weeks went by. Jim didn't soften on his position. Roadblocks kept popping up to prevent my dream from happening. Jim and I had many conversations in the milking parlor while he was milking about processing our own milk. One conversation sticks in my mind. After pressing Jim to commit to the idea, he responded, "I'm not borrowing another damn dime."

Was Jim right? We had already poured our hearts and souls into the farm, and for what? More and more debt with no hope? Was Granddad really right when he said to sell the blankety-blank-farm at the top of his lungs that day in the cabin yard? Trying to keep the farm as a dairy farm was feeling more like a curse, not a blessing. How many sacrifices had to be made by our families to keep the dairy open?

There were more questions than answers. But I simply wasn't ready to let the dairy go and let down all the Hatchers preceding me who had worked so hard to keep the dairy farm. William, Abram, George, and Abe Hatcher had persevered and held on to the farm despite the Civil War, World War I, World War II, the Great Depression, and much back-breaking work and worry. Why couldn't I persevere as well?

I wanted to give the same opportunity to my kids and grandkids that had been afforded to me by my granddad and my dad: to grow up, live, work, play, and die on a working dairy. I couldn't stomach the idea of being the Hatcher that closed the dairy. One thing was for sure, though—we had to do something different. What we were doing was absolutely not working, was not sustainable, and entailed more going out than coming in.

I called MTSU back. To sweeten the pot, my last offer was for us, the farm, to buy them a bottler—a filler for plastic jugs—and donate it to them since they did not have one. MTSU was currently only putting milk in a bag that was placed in a dispenser to supply their cafeteria. We needed our milk bottled in milk jugs to supply customers and retailers. Several weeks later, MTSU called me back. After looking into the idea a little more closely, they felt they could do it after all. The bottler would give MTSU the opportunity to bottle their milk and market it on campus.

This was a way for us to test the market with little investment in equipment up-front. After the donation of the bottler, the only costs would be for milk hauling and processing expenses, allowing us to avoid sinking a pile of money into the project.

Later that evening in Jim's office, the milking parlor, I told Jim that MTSU had called and agreed to bottle our milk under certain conditions, I said, "We either need to sell out or bottle our own milk. Sharon and I are going to do this; are you in or out?"

Without a moment's pause in his milking, he replied, "I don't know. I'll let you know in the morning." I fully expected him to say no the next morning, but much to my surprise, he said, "I'm in." Our lives would never be the same.

Chapter Eighteen

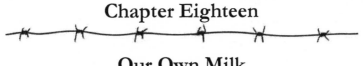

Our Own Milk

Now the real work started. We negotiated a short-term pilot marketing agreement with MTSU for them to process one hundred fifty loads of our milk in exchange for the donation of a bottler that would do the job. We would also cover any related transportation and processing expenses for our milk. A load was defined as up to a full load on their one-ton, blue 1985 *Ford* truck, which had a four-hundred-gallon milk tank mounted on the back. The tank held about thirty-four hundred pounds of milk when completely full. Now the task was to try to find a small enough bottler to fit into the limited space of the processing facility at MTSU.

The problem was that small bottlers are pretty much nonexistent in North America. Australia, New Zealand, and some European countries, where small processors are plentiful, are where all the small bottlers are.

I went online searching for the bottler with just the right footprint to fit in the corner that would be dedicated for that purpose at MTSU's creamery. One particular company from New Zealand that handled all kinds of processing equipment for small processors caught my attention. I decided to give them a call. The fellow on the other end of the line was really helpful, friendly, and had the coolest accent. After several weeks of bantering back and forth, we arrived on a deal with a company half-way across the world. The deal was for the bottler to be shipped over to Tennessee. Since neither we nor MTSU had any experience with a filler or bottler, the most important part of the deal was for one of their company representatives to fly over once the filler arrived in order to install it and train us on its use.

Besides supplying the customer with an excellent quality product, the most important part of marketing a product is the label on the product. Jim has a good friend, Daryl Stevens, who is talented in graphics design. We recruited him to design a label for us. What should we call this new business venture? To me, it was crucial to include the Hatcher name and the word *family* on the label because this really was going to be a family initiative; thus, Hatcher Family Dairy was chosen.

The Hatcher Family Dairy logo Daryl created was a thing of beauty and genius. It looked earthy, old fashioned, and unassuming, but also bold. We were on our way with this new adventure. Hatcher Family Dairy was born.

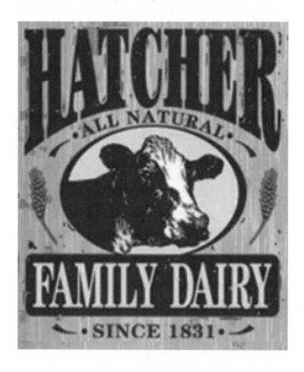

Coincidentally, around that time, *Whole Foods*—the organic, all-natural grocery store chain—was holding an informational meeting for local farmers that might be interested in marketing their products at *Whole Foods*. A new *Whole Foods* store was under construction in Green Hills in Nashville. They needed local suppliers in a few months. Daryl got together a Hatcher Family Dairy promotional packet including a colorful product sales sheet we intended to carry: whole milk, cream, two-percent, skim, and chocolate milk.

We felt that offering whole milk that was non-homogenized, with cream rising to the top, would set us apart from traditional homogenized milk. Milk naturally comes from the cow non-homogenized. Homogenization is a mechanical process that disrupts the fat globules and evenly distributes the fat into the milk, preventing the cream from rising to the top.

Realizing that some people don't like to deal with the clumps of cream in their milk and that still others want no fat at all, we made homogenized two-percent and skim milk part of our offering. Our chocolate milk would be a full-fat, best-taste-ever, just-plain-good product—the world's best chocolate milk. At that point, though, all of this was just an idea on paper; we hadn't actually bottled the first jug of milk yet.

Sharon and I signed in at the meeting and awaited our turn to see the grocery buyer for *Whole Foods*, Big Daddy. A huge crowd of farmers was in attendance, all hoping for a chance to market their products with *Whole Foods*. We waited about an hour until our name was called to see Big Daddy, who turned out to not be big at all. He was a solidly built, muscular, and jolly man.

I gave Big Daddy my sales pitch, pushing us as a local, farm family with a pasture-based dairy. He glanced through the promotional packet with interest, looking at the Hatcher Family Dairy logo and the mocked up photos of the products we hoped to soon offer, and said, "When we open, we will take all the milk you can supply us." I was stunned. There was certainly motivation for us now to keep pressing on.

Almost all the farms that I had visited sold at least some of their milk directly from their farm. I thought it was important to have a milk store on our farm. The county in which we live has an income per capita per household as high as anywhere in the United States. The population of Williamson County, along with both housing and community development, is exploding. Our county has a county commission and a planning commission to help control the growth.

Hatcher Family Dairy happened to be the first in the county to want to set up an on-the-farm store to market agricultural products. The current regulations on the books limited the size of an on-farm market to three hundred fifty square feet. In addition, the store had to be under the roof line of our existing vet clinic at the same location on the farm.

Sharon and I attended countless county commission meetings, planning commission meetings, and public hearings, all to state our case for what seemed like what might be an unattainable dream. However, our local commissioners and community rose up in support of our plan. In the end, the county granted us approval and also made many changes that improved the regulations for direct marketing of one's own agricultural products from one's farm in our county. Our initiative had paved the way for other farmers in our county to direct sell their farm products to consumers.

We followed all the county guidelines for constructing our farm milk store as part of the existing veterinary clinic building. Sharon designed the small store with a country theme. The farm store was constructed with a wooden front porch that matched the clinic, a small display area, a large marble checkout counter, and a six-door, glass-front display cooler for the milk. The compressor for the cooler was purchased new because we didn't want any trouble cooling the milk. We wanted a patio to provide an acceptable access to the front porch and also to serve as some outside seating for customers.

I thought it would be nice to have a rock patio. After all, I reasoned, we had plenty of limestone and sandstone rock on the farm. It should be easy. However, I had no idea what I was getting into. For weeks I collected beautiful rock of all sizes and interesting shapes from all over the farm, in the creek, in the fields, from the fence rows, in the woods, and in the ditches, accumulating a massive rock inventory. Some of the rocks were huge, requiring me to load them carefully with the frontend loader of the tractor.

I had no experience laying rock, so I enlisted the help of a landscaper friend, Scott Powers, to consult on the project. We planned a rock wall around the towering oak tree by the veterinary clinic front entrance and a thirty-five by thirty-five foot patio in front of the milk store entrance. Scott showed me how to make a good foundation and how to lay and level the rock for the wall in front of the clinic.

I did most of the work on the store patio myself, laying each rock with care. Each one was unique in color, shape, and size, and had its own story for me. I worked on the patio project on evenings and weekends for months.

Once, one of the large limestone rocks shifted in the frontend loader as I was unloading it. It mashed the end of the middle finger on my right hand, splitting the flesh and soaking my gloved hand with bright red blood. I lost my fingernail over the course of several weeks. The finger eventually healed, but the accident left an obvious mark on my finger for at least a year.

The rock patio was one of the hardest things I have ever done in my life. I'm extremely proud of it. It was something I built with my own hands that will be there for a long time, reminding me of the kind of hard work Mr. Tomlin, Mr. Pagel, and Mr. York did every day for all their lives.

After what seemed like an eternity but was really only a few months, the bottler finally arrived at MTSU. Then there were several weeks more before I picked the consultant up from the airport. I had just finished the patio at the milk store, and the county had given us the go-ahead to open the store. The New Zealand consultant had a total of three working days to set up the bottler and train us to run it. The filler was set up the first day, water was used the second day to practice filling the bottles, and Hatcher milk was finally bottled on the third day.

The question that came up was how much milk we should bottle. As hard as I had tried, the only local store that had given me a firm commitment to sell our milk that first week was College Grove grocery. None of the chain grocery stores would even consider working with us except *Whole Foods*, and they weren't open yet. The only other outlets for the sale of our milk that first week were the *Franklin Farmers Market* that Saturday and the milk store on the farm.

We ended up bottling about two hundred gallons of milk that first time because we were too scared to do more for fear of not being able to sell it. The bottling was finished around nine that night at MTSU. The bottled milk then had to be hauled back to the farm store in our recently acquired refrigerated truck to be hand-labeled. Jim had acquired the delivery truck somewhere in Alabama or Georgia.

Once back at the store, the first of many hand-labeling parties began with all available Hatchers and all the in-laws and the outlaws of the family we could muster, working together like drones until the job was completed just before one o'clock in the morning, May 16, 2007. Attendance at these milk labeling parties, of which this was only the first, usually included Jim and his girlfriend, Jorie, my nephew Will with his wife Becca, my wife Sharon, my son Charles, my daughter Jennifer, my sister Lucy with her husband Dave and daughter Jessica, Lucy's first husband Chubby and his wife Kim, and our good friend Norman Giller with his daughter Rebecca.

My son Charles said that someday we would have an automated labeling machine even if he had to buy one himself.

There would be two people who hauled the milk from the truck into the store and to the five or six people sitting at tables and labeling the full milk jugs. All available tables and chairs at the store would be used to label the milk. We had it down to a science, an assembly line of perfection; everyone had a job and knew how to do it well. We had food at the hand-labeling parties, either potluck, store-delivered pizza, or sandwiches left over from the store. The hand-labeling parties gave the family a chance to spend valuable time together on a weekly basis, something that's often absent from America's families today. Despite the fun that we had together, it was still a chore to label all the milk once a week on Tuesday nights, especially if processing breakdowns occurred, which would delay the completion of the hand-labeling until the wee hours of the morning.

The day after the first hand-labeling party, the first half

gallons and pints of our milk were proudly displayed in the cooler at our milk store. I made the first delivery ever of Hatcher milk to College Grove grocery myself. This was the beginning of the Hatcher Family Dairy. I was ecstatic, proudly loading the milk onto the refrigerated shelf. Now what? Would people actually buy the milk and what should we do with rest of the milk we had just processed?

On a wing and a prayer, I took some of our milk to the *Franklin Farmers Market* the following Saturday. I had no prior marketing experience of any kind, nor had I ever been to the *Franklin Farmers Market* before. I set up a table in my assigned booth space. Half-gallons and pints of Hatcher milk were attractively displayed on ice in a galvanized metal wash tub.

Customers browsed up and down the aisles, stopping and talking with farmers at the booths along the way. It came easily to me as I answered questions about our farm and milk. We had a story to tell and I knew it well. Bottling our own milk was our final attempt to make the farm sustainable and to save it; that was my message. 'Hatcher Family Dairy: Since 1831' is on every label, and we want everyone to know our story.

One fellow asked me that morning, "What's so special about your milk?"

I told him, "It's produced in a pasture/grass based system by Hatcher cows, on Hatcher land that has been in the family now for six generations. The milk is fresh, sometimes being bottled the same day the cow is milked."

Then he said, "Give me a half gallon of whole milk with the cream on the top, a half-gallon of the chocolate milk, and a pint of cream."

That was the way it went the rest of the morning. When it was time to close, I had no milk to load back up and take home. I really felt good about how well our milk was received that first Saturday at the *Franklin Farmers Market*. I was beginning to think this just might work.

Hatcher Family Dairy began to grow, one customer at a time and by word of mouth, from that day forward. The Saturday *Franklin Farmers Market* is open year-round, winter and summer alike. Hatchers have only missed one or two Saturdays since we started there in 2007—one Saturday due to snow and one Saturday because the delivery truck broke down. The market has grown tremendously and so has the Hatcher Family Dairy. The *Franklin Farmers Market* has been one of the keys to our success.

Our milk drinkers began to tell us things about our milk, like "It has a good flavor" or "It keeps longer in the refrigerator than other milk" or "I can tell by the taste of your milk when you rotate your cows onto a fresh pasture lot."

One old man who walked with a cane looked me right in the eye once and said, "This whole milk with the cream on top takes me back sixty years when we milked our family cow by hand and stored the milk in the ice box."

People began to recognize our milk products as quality products. Word spread about Hatcher Milk even though we never spent any money on advertising. We were unsuccessful after multiple attempts in getting Hatcher milk in any chain grocery stores other than *Whole Foods*, but mom-and-pop grocery stores, rural country stores, and coffee shops began to call, wanting our milk.

Instead of processing one old blue truckload of our milk per week at MTSU, we began to process two loads a week to keep up with demand. It was becoming readily apparent that bottling our own milk was the right thing to do. Jim was learning how to operate all the processing equipment at MTSU's small facility, including the separator, homogenizer, pasteurizer, and bottler; he was becoming really good at it. The pilot marketing agreement had served its purpose—we now knew we should build our own creamery on the farm to bottle our milk.

It was time to start planning again. We simultaneously applied for a USDA grant that matched working capital for value-added dairy products and started discussions again with Williamson County Planning Commission about building a creamery. Permission was granted to build the creamery after another public hearing, another public notice, and a permit being issued by the Tennessee Department of Environment and Conservation for the discharge of waste water from the creamery into our concrete lagoon. The waste water would be mixed with the watery cow manure and used for irrigation and fertilization as part of the farm nutrient management plan.

We made many costly mistakes when building the creamery, which was built close to the milk barn so that raw milk could be easily pumped over from the milk barn's raw-milk storage tank. When we started, we thought we could build it for around $550,000, but we ended up spending half again more than that. An unanticipated cost came in the form of a drop ceiling, made from waterproof board, which had to be put in to meet pasteurized milk ordinance standards. The original plan was for the floor to be concrete with an epoxy paint covering, but the concrete was not sloped adequately to drain, so it had to be redone with sand under tile to correct the slope.

We constructed and completed a concrete dock to load the milk only to find out that the dock didn't meet regulations and couldn't be used. It seemed like one thing after another was going wrong. I had to go back to the lenders three times for more money until they finally said, "That's it; you can't borrow any more money!"

In spite of all of the setbacks, at the end of March 2009, the creamery was finally permitted by the Tennessee Department of Agriculture as a dairy processing facility.

The new *Whole Foods* in Green Hills was ready to open,

more stores wanted our milk, and the USDA grant had been approved. We needed every available Hatcher to work in our growing business. Sharon managed the farm store. Jim managed the creamery. Beth's son Willie delivered the milk. My sister Lucy came aboard for public relations, farmers markets, and managing the farm tours. My son Charles was still in college, awaiting graduation in May, but was farming, helping with deliveries, and milking when he could. Charles did get that automatic labeling machine that he wanted after all, but didn't have to buy it himself.

We all missed the socialization the weekly family and friends labeling parties provided, but we certainly did not miss the hand-labeling of several hundred gallons of milk per week. Jim had his hands full as the creamery manager. It took time for Jim to master the processing of our milk in our new creamery. Problems with the separator, the bottler, and cooler compressors persisted for several months.

Sometimes a simple part or a valve would malfunction, causing us to delay processing of the milk until the part came in and messing up the delivery schedule for the whole week. Nothing was cheap. The creamery is a sea of expensive stainless-steel pipes, tanks, fillers, and valves. A small stainless-steel valve might cost a thousand dollars. Jim has a keen mind for mechanical and engineering-type processes, and by the end of six months he had the creamery running like a finely-tuned instrument.

Whole Foods had their long-awaited grand opening in Green Hills. Our milk was prominently displayed in the dairy section with photos of Hatcher Family members, including our cows, directly at eye level for all customers to see.

We had received requests for our milk to be bottled in gallons for some time. Once the new creamery was done, our whole milk cream line, two-percent, and skim were bottled in gallon jugs. Our milk sales began to steadily increase week by week, thanks in large part to *Whole Foods*. When I saw my first gallon of Hatcher milk in a shopping cart at *Whole Foods*, my heart swelled with pride again.

A few months later, my daughter was in the *Whole Foods* Green Hills location one day checking out with a few items at the clerk's counter. The clerk happened to notice she was wearing a Hatcher Family Dairy shirt and asked her, "Do you know the Hatchers?"

Jennifer responded, "I am a Hatcher."

The girl somewhat surprised said, "Wow, that's so cool!"

Hatchers were now elevated to rock star status.

Our customers had identified us as the farmers behind the milk that they were drinking. We had earned the trust of our milk drinkers. They knew that if we put our name on it, it was going to be good and it came from Hatcher animals on the Hatcher farm.

Whole Foods acquired all *Wild Oats* groceries nationally in 2009. The *Wild Oats* store in Cool Springs became a *Whole Foods* store, and we started delivering Hatcher milk there as well. The dairy buyer at *Whole Foods* in Memphis found out about our milk from the other *Whole Foods* buyers, and he wanted our milk also. The *Whole Foods* in Cool Springs agreed to let us drop-ship the Memphis *Whole Foods* milk order there to be transported to Memphis by *Whole Foods* trucks. We now had three *Whole Foods* store accounts in Tennessee. Business was booming.

Jim had acquired one used refrigerated delivery truck just before we started bottling, but we really needed another one. If the one truck we had broke down, deliveries would be stopped until the truck was repaired. A pretty nice used truck became available at a reasonable price from a home-delivery grocery business going out of business. We bought the truck. Jim made some minor repairs and applied the vinyl Hatcher Family Dairy signage—designed by Jim's graphic design friend Daryl—to the entire sides of both trucks. The side of each truck showed old 1500—one of the Hall of Famers—grazing red clover in a field on the hill next to the everlasting spring.

Whole Foods built a brand-new store just off Interstate 65 north of Franklin that was no more than eleven miles from us. The old store in Cool Springs was closed. This store was its replacement. It was much larger, with more amenities. After a few months, our sales at the new location doubled compared to the old store.

My nephew Will had been taking care of the milk deliveries up until this point. In 2011, he accepted a full time job with a chance of advancement at the same *Nissan* plant his dad had worked all those years after the USDA grant expired. After graduating from MTSU in May of 2009, Charles had decided to stay on the farm and use his agriculture business degree to advance the family business. Charles was therefore able to take over the management of the delivery routes that Will had established so well. I was extremely proud of him.

Lucy was uniquely qualified to be the farm spokesperson, the face of the farm, and farm tour director because of her background in modeling and acting as well as her communication skills. Hatcher Family Dairy had been featured on local television, the local newspaper, and multiple agricultural magazines. By popular demand, Lucy went on a speaking tour of sorts, speaking at business luncheons, conventions, and agricultural clubs. She preached on the basic tenants of farm and Hatcher Family Dairy: local, farm fresh, family, heritage, and sustainability.

Requests were coming in for farm tours. People wanted to see where Hatcher milk came from. We attended some agri-tourism conferences and visited farms that were giving tours to learn more about how we should conduct tours on our farm. We settled on educational tours of our working farm, focusing on the production of Hatcher milk all the way through, from the cow to the Hatcher milk drinker.

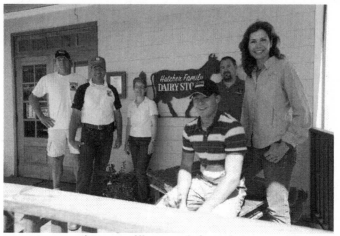

**At our milk store-left to right,
Jim, myself, Sharon, Charles, Will and Lucy.**

The tour became a walking tour starting at our milk store. It currently consists of multiple tour stations or stops, including the dry cow lot (where the heavy pregnant cows and heifers are kept), weaned calf lots, nursery area, milk barn, and creamery. The final stop is back at the store for a taste of our milk.

Many people have enjoyed these tours: home schoolers, public-school groups, veterans, grandparents, and all manner of city folks. The farm tours are our best way to educate people and to promote our products. Once people take a farm tour, most are converted for life. There have been many children raised on Hatcher milk after taking a farm tour. Most become addicted to our milk because of the flavor and taste. Our milk tastes creamier, with more body and a bolder flavor, than regular grocery store milk because of our cows' predominately grass-based diet.

Both Lucy and her husband Dave worked on the farm

along with the rest of us as a family unit. Dave helped Will with the deliveries and was also instrumental on milk processing day as he was trained to run the separator. The separator is the machine with multiple parts that spins like a centrifuge to pull the cream off the milk.

Unexpectedly, Lucy and Dave went through a difficult divorce in 2013. This was a dark time on the farm affecting all of us as we witnessed the pain first hand. The pain inflicted by the divorce left Lucy feeling like her heart and lungs had been ripped out of her chest. Recovery for Lucy involved a clean break from the farm to pursue her first love, horses, but also to re-energize her lifelong modeling career. She could make more money in a day's modeling than in a month working on the farm. Lucy's departure from the business was a big loss. Charles and Sharon assumed the tour and public relation responsibilities in addition to their already-busy schedules.

Chapter Nineteen

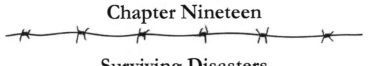

Surviving Disasters

The 1000-year Flood

Farmers are constantly at the mercy of Mother Nature, and Hatcher Family Dairy is no exception in being vulnerable to her periodic mood swings. The first in a series of extreme weather events occurred a few years after our on farm creamery opened in 2009, taking the farm and all those on it to our breaking point.

On Saturday, May 1st, and Sunday, May 2nd, of 2010, an unprecedented, monumental rain event took place in Middle Tennessee. In less than forty-eight hours, over thirteen inches of rain fell on the farm. By late Sunday afternoon, rushing white water flowed in the small valley just off our back porch. A newly created river flowed between our house and the small pond above it, crossing the cow path to the milk barn behind the upright silo.

As the milk cows descended off the hill on the cow path for the evening milking, they immediately balked when encountering deep rushing rapids. Milking was delayed about three hours until the water subsided to a point at which the water level—at the level of the cows' hocks—was low enough for the cows to cross. Other than the milking delay and the severe erosion of the steep part of Jennifer's driveway going up on the hill, the farm was spared for the most part. There was no loss of life or property.

Unfortunately, Nashville and other parts of Middle Tennessee were not so lucky. Some areas received rainfall totals of over twenty inches, resulting in loss of life and tremendous, unprecedented property damage. Downtown Nashville, Opry Mills, subdivisions, and the hardest-hit areas sustained catastrophic flood damage, even total destruction for some, resulting in millions and millions of dollars in losses. Countless buildings and properties were condemned or could not be rebuilt at the same location as a result of the flood.

Hoping to help in some small way, Lucy, Sharon, Charles, and I took a load of free milk to one of the devastated neighborhoods in Franklin the next weekend. Passing out the milk to deeply appreciative recipients was one of the most satisfying experiences of my life. The Tennessee flood of 2010 became known as the 1000-year flood because a flood of this magnitude was only supposed to happen once in a 1000 years. The 1000-year flood changed the course of many lives forever.

The Great Drought of 2012

Mother's Day of 2012 was much like previous Mother's Days. After church, we went to see Mom back up on Nathan Smith Hollow in her cottage to wish her a Happy Mother's Day and to show our appreciation for her in raising us. There was a nice rain falling, evidenced by the soothing sound of the rain hitting the tin roof of the cabin. We had no idea that this would be the last time we would hear that sound for a long time—we would have no more measurable accumulation of rain for months. It was Sunday, May 13, 2012.

The farm relies heavily on spring/summer grasses, both for the cows to graze and also to make hay to feed the cows during the cold days of the winter when the pasture is not growing much. By the end of May or the first week of June, all the hay had been harvested for the spring. It still hadn't rained since the 13th, but we really didn't think that much of it.

Cows enjoy a variety of forages, but one of the favorite

forages of our cows is corn silage. Corn silage is the fermented product created by chopping the whole corn plant during its immature stage, when the plant is green and the kernels of corn are bursting with milky sweetness. Our cows are fed some corn silage during the winter months or during drought periods when grass is not abundant. Fermented silage gives off aromas similar to beer, whiskey, and candy. Cows love corn silage. It smells so good to me, I'm often tempted to pick up a handful of corn silage and chew on it.

The corn silage is stored in a concrete ground silo until it's needed for feeding the cows. It's then loaded with a tractor front-end loader onto a feed wagon. The feed wagon is taken to the paddock the cows are lounging in when the pasture is not lush enough to meet the nutritional requirements of the cows. We had planted the corn the last week of April in the big field next to the everlasting spring and the field across from Jennifer's house for our 2012 corn silage crop. The corn sprouted soon after planting. The stand appeared to be good. The Mother's Day rain further advanced our hopes of a good corn silage crop.

The milk deliveries had grown to the point now that Charles needed some help. Our organic-produce neighbors, the Delvins, acquired a new son-in-law with experience in growing produce, but they couldn't absorb him into their current operation. His name was Brandon. Brandon was a very likeable young man with curly red hair and a distinguished half-growth beard. He needed employment. We needed someone who could work, so we hired him.

Charles put him to work immediately making deliveries in the second truck. Brandon gleefully completed his delivery route obligations and was interested in doing more on the farm. Even though he had no previous animal care experience, we added to his responsibilities the cleaning and feeding of the calves in the nursery area. Brandon could be found talking to the calves and affectionately stroking them just because he liked them. The calves liked Brandon, too. Brandon enjoyed caring for the calves so much that he could be seen gleefully tiptoeing around the calf area as if gliding in air like *Dr. Seuss' Grinch.*

Although Brandon was enjoying his work, he missed growing vegetables. I decided to give him the opportunity to grow vegetables on our farm. We picked out two small plots of ground on the farm for Brandon to grow vegetables on. One plot of about one and a half acres was behind the tobacco barn and the other plot of about one half acre was below the old pond on Aunt Martha's side of the farm. This plot was near the large oak trees that I had carved my initials into as a kid. The soil was unexpectedly rich, dark, and fertile—so rich, loose, and deep, in fact, that Brandon sunk the plow and cultivator down to the top of the shanks, shearing some of the bolts. His tractor moaned, straining to pull the equipment through the deep loamy soil. Brandon said he had never seen soil quite so good.

The plot behind the tobacco barn had been used to grow burley tobacco over twenty-five years earlier. The only use for the ground since that time had been to graze cattle. I think the reason for such good soil conditions was the secret ingredient of cow manure. Over the years, the cows had naturally applied their own manure on the soil, and Brandon had recently emptied the liquid manure contents of the entire lagoon by pump irrigation onto the plots as well.

The soil was in perfect condition for the vegetables to be planted. Rows and rows of tomato plants were set out first, followed by eggplant and cucumbers in the one-acre plot behind the tobacco barn. The whole process was repeated in the smaller plot about thirty days later to provide for a longer harvest period.

As an experienced produce farmer, Brandon knew his produce crop had to be irrigated to be most productive. He installed a drip-irrigation system under black plastic for the produce, piggy-backing off our existing in-ground PVP pipe system that ran from the concrete waste lagoon. He used two water sources for the irrigation, the big pond down at the bottom of the hill next to the milk barn for the large plot and the old pond below the terrace lot for the smaller plot. A large, gas-powered pump on wheels was placed below the large pond. A large, soft hose was laid on top of the ground, connecting the pump over to the in-ground pipe system. The pump was powerful enough to push the pond water over a half a mile through the in-ground pipe system to the plot behind the tobacco barn. A pressure reducer had to be installed just ahead of the drip irrigation system to lower the pressure and allow the drip irrigation to work properly.

All was well. We had a good stand of corn for corn silage. Our farm's first experience with growing produce was off to a great start. By the middle of June, though, we were becoming increasingly aware that the farm was becoming dry. By the end of June, it was evident we were in a drought. Brandon was purposely drip-irrigating his produce plots once or twice a week. Drip irrigation does not require a large volume of water. The produce was looking really good. However, the leaves of our small corn plants were beginning to twist, demonstrating their need for water.

Days turned into weeks and weeks turned into months with still no rain in sight; we were in the middle of the worst drought I had seen in my lifetime. All the ponds, even the ones that Brandon wasn't pumping from, were dramatically low. I became obsessed with the weather. I was an addict to my cell phone *Weather Channel* App, checking the radar every hour to look for a rain shower that might reach the farm. I began coveting our neighbor's rainfall. Sometimes it would rain just over the hill but not on our farm.

When it seemed things couldn't get any worse, Jennifer called to let me know that they had no water at her house on the hill. The everlasting spring hadn't dried up, but the water coming out of the side of the hill and going into the sediment tank had reduced down to a stream the size of your little finger. The spring reservoir water level had dropped below the inlet of the submersible pump at the bottom of the reservoir, causing the pump to shut off. As a result, Jennifer and Chuck had no water, and neither did the big concrete water trough at the top of the hill that watered the milk cows.

In order for Jennifer and Chuck to have water on the hill, we connected the concrete water trough on the hill to the well at Granddad's log cabin. After forty-eight hours without the cows being watered from the everlasting spring, Jennifer and Chuck had water again. For two days they bathed at Sharon's parent's house because Gabaga and Parker had city water. By this time in the drought, the city water was restricted as well, with no washing of cars or watering lawns allowed.

At the bottom of the hill, the water level in the big pond that Brandon was irrigating from, which the milk cows were obtaining water from by gravity flow, was becoming dangerously low. Over the months, as Brandon had irrigated the produce plots, the pond water level had dropped so low that the top of the big cedar post holding the gravity flow pipe to the floor of the pond became gradually exposed. Fearing that we would run out of pond water to water the milk cows, I told Brandon he was under a water use restriction too. He could pump no more than once a week for a few hours.

As a stop-gap measure, we pumped all the water from the two small ponds into the big pond below, buying us some time. In the days that followed, we began to experience low water pressure from the well at the cabin after regular use of water. After waiting several hours for the well to catch up, the water pressure would return to a normal level. The everlasting spring that had never gone dry might actually be going dry, all the ponds were within a few feet of being empty if not already empty, the creek running through the lower valley of the farm was completely dry, and the well at the cabin seemed to be limited.

The actual outside temperature reached a record 109° F. The sun and heat further parched the already scorched earth. We found out later that 2012 was the second warmest year on record for the Middle Tennessee area. In a final desperate attempt to save the pitiful cactus-looking corn crop, Brandon showed us how to drip-irrigate five acres of the corn, but it was too little too late. The drip-irrigation system could not deliver enough water to the thirsty, drought-stricken corn to save it.

I feared that if it didn't rain soon, we would have no water anywhere to water the livestock. In desperation, I called a well-digging company to come out and dig a well. I knew that across the road, Laurel Cove had dug several wells with good success, some wells yielding as much as several hundred gallons per minute; maybe we could be as lucky. After all, there is no better time to drill a well than during a drought. If you hit water, you know it's going to be a reliable well.

The well digger used a fruit-tree wishbone branch to witch for water on the farm. The branch pulled heavily to the ground just below my house to the north of the milk barn. I was feeling good about our chances to hit a good stream of water. The well digger hit 7.5 gallons of water flow by sixty feet. We were hoping to have a well capable of irrigating our pitiful corn, but this wasn't near enough water. Five thousand dollars' worth of drilling later, we were at a depth of three hundred and fifty feet with the same flow of 7.5 gallons of water.

We weren't complaining, but we were disappointed; there was no chance of having enough water to irrigate. However, the new well was good enough to provide water for five water troughs for the livestock with enough left over to spray out the milking parlor and holding pen during cleanup. Under our present drought conditions, this was a blessing. The new well gave us a dependable water source at a time when we needed it the most.

The drilling must have hit a pocket of natural gas, because hazy fumes billowed up from the well casing to about eight or ten inches into the air. One could hear the release of gas coming from the well casing. It sounded like propane or a welding torch after it was lit. The well digger said the gas would go away, and after a few weeks it did.

By this stage of the drought, the corn as well as all the pastures appeared to be a total loss. The sick, greenish-yellow, twisted corn plants looked like cacti in the middle of desert. The corn plants ranged from waist-high to no more than a few inches. Charles said we would be in good shape if the cows could eat cacti. It made me physically ill to look at the corn fields.

USDA confirmed by a site visit that the corn crop was a total loss. All our once-green pastures were now brown, and there were large cracks in the ground from the dryness and heat. Dusty conditions prevailed, visually re-creating the early construction days of Laurel Cove as a constant reminder of the drought. When the cows were being gathered to be milked, a billowing dust bowl followed the cows to the holding pen.

And so it went, each day the same as the previous, over and over again, just like in the movie *Groundhog Day*, with still no rain. We woke up each and every morning to the same thing: dust, scorching heat, brown grass, and brown corn. The meteorologist would report a ten percent chance of rain or no rain chance at all every single day in the ten day forecast, maddening me further. I felt like Job of biblical fame. Was this a test of faith? Was God trying to tell me something?

Although Brandon didn't think so at the time, his produce crop was doing extremely well. The tomatoes looked like they were grown by the *Jolly Green Giant*. But harvest was near, and if they didn't get necessary water right here at the critical end of the growing period, he could have a crop failure, too.

Everyone on the farm was depressed, even the cows. They looked down at the scant brown grass and back up again as if to say they didn't sign up for this. Since the corn could not be chopped for silage, we pondered on what to do with it. We could bush-hog it down and get nothing out of it, or we could try something we had never done before and cut it like as if it were hay. That last option is what we decided on. We cut the corn plants with the hay mower, raked them with the hay rake, rolled them into big bales with the hay baler, and made baleage out of it all by wrapping the bales in plastic with a balewrapper leased from a neighbor friend.

The forty acres of corn made a dismal one hundred bales of the drought-stricken corn baleage. The bales fermented for about a week before we started feeding them to the cows at the rate of one to two bales a day. Surprising enough, it wasn't bad feed. The cows liked it, although milk production was down. But after a few weeks, since the cows had no green grass to graze, we had depleted all our recently acquired baleage, and the spring hay reserves were nearly depleted too. I was at my lowest low. There was nothing else I could do. I could only control the controllable, and this drought was out of my control. That's when it occurred to me like a ton of bricks falling on me: God was in control. I was not. I had placed the farm at a higher level than my faith. God had sent a message through the drought—nothing comes before Him, not even the farm.

It took the drought to force me to realize that anything on this earth can be taken away from you in an instant. The only thing you really have at all times is God. I had been token-praying during the whole drought, but not fervently. After being completely broken down by the drought and realizing I wasn't in control, I began to pray fervently, giving it up to God for Him to handle and putting Him first. Only then did things begin to improve. I never felt stronger. Only when you become your weakest can you become your strongest.

My son-in-law, Chuck, met a young farmer at a Farm Bureau Young Farmers and Ranchers meeting named Brandon Whitt during the drought. He was a nice young man in his early thirties who operated a hog and cropping farm for his in-laws in the next county east of us. With an unassuming smile, Brandon offered to help us out of our current dire circumstance. His corn was deeply affected by the drought as well, but not as severely as ours. His corn was not good enough to be harvested for shelled corn. The best option for him was to chop it for corn silage into large plastic bags on his farm. Brandon offered to sell us about four hundred tons of the corn silage for a very reasonable price. This was enough corn silage to at least get us until the end of the year. Brandon began to haul the corn silage over to us in his big grain truck as we needed it. I like to think of Brandon as our little angel sent by God to deliver us from the drought.

We started feeding Brandon's corn silage to the cows immediately, going through a truckload of it every four to five days. Brandon helped us even more by selling us over forty large roll bales of excellent-quality, fine Bermuda grass hay that he had harvested in the spring before the drought. The hay was fed to the cows as well. They ate every stem of the hay that we put in the roll bale feeders.

Within days after Brandon started delivering the corn silage, it began to rain. The first shower yielded almost an inch of rain, then a second shower and a third shower came until over the course of four days we had a total accumulation of 2.8 inches. It was the end of July. The farm had gone through a two-and-a-half-month drought period without any significant rainfall. The ground soaked up the much-needed rain like a sponge, leaving no runoff to fill the ponds. Jim immediately planted all the recently harvested, drought-stricken corn fields with wheat and triticale. The seed sprouted almost instantaneously, providing the first hopeful sign of greener pastures to come.

Brandon's produce crop turned out to be the best he had ever seen for tomatoes, cucumbers, and eggplant. He hauled truckloads of the abundant, beautiful vegetables off the hill to be marketed to anxious retailers.

The drought had taken its toll on all of us. Brandon said even though this produce crop was the best he ever had, the pressure was too great to bear emotionally; he would never do it again. Financially, the drought had proven to be devastating for the farm. We had effectively paid double for all our forages. We paid twice for pasture, twice for hay, and twice for corn silage.

I'm not sure whether the drought was actually a test or not. In the end, the farm did survive. The drought taught all of us a lesson; it sure taught me that what doesn't kill you does make you stronger. I'm stronger spiritually now than ever for going through the drought. There is a God. I'm sure of it.

It wasn't until Sunday, January 13, 2013, that the drought felt truly over to me. A flash flood warning had been issued for our area. Severe downpours were predicted shortly. Sharon said, "Let's go ahead and start the evening feeding early to beat the rain." Sharon and I both donned our new rain suits, complete with top-coat, hoods, and bottom pants. I headed out the door to deliver roll bale hay to the heifers' groups and milk cows on the *John Deere 4020*. The hay spear was mounted on the three-point hitch on the rear of the tractor.

Sharon was going to feed the chickens, gather the eggs, feed the sheep behind the house, and then feed the sheep at Aunt Martha's and the twin goats at the clinic. I got halfway up the hill on the tractor to deliver the hay when the bottom fell out. The heavens opened up. The rain came down torrentially in sheets, lowering my visibility to near-zero. I begin to notice that water was running down my rain-pant legs into my boots, but I didn't care. I was so glad to see the rain that I was perfectly content to have my boots filled up with rain water.

By the time I delivered the hay to the milk cows on the hill and headed back down the hill on the tractor, water was pouring down the driveway in the tire tracks like a river. You may have heard of a gully washer—that is what this was. All the rain water from all the hills on both sides of the driveway was feeding into Jim's five-pond system.

Previous to this rain, none of the ponds had reached their pre-drought levels, especially the big pond. The top of the cedar post at the bottom of the big pond was still visible. In a matter of minutes, that began to change. The top pond filled first and each pond below it began to fill in succession. Although the heavy rain had mostly stopped by dark, by the next morning, rain water was still flowing off the hill from all directions. Jennifer's driveway up the hill was deeply rutted, but the big pond was finally full at long last, nearly eight months after the drought had begun.

Some say the drought was the worst in fifty to sixty years. I was glad the drought was finally over and looked forward to a normal growing season in the spring. The cows were, too. I'm hoping it will be the last severe drought in my lifetime, unless God decides to teach me another lesson.

"Do all a mule can do"

After the drought of 2012, Brandon—our main delivery guy— left to pursue growing produce full time. Providence directed a series of outstanding young men to work at Hatcher Family Dairy when we needed help the most. They were: brothers Casey and Cameron Harmon, young Dave—known as 'Davo,' the improbable redneck from California—and Brian, the patriot.

The Harmon brothers are the grandsons of our good

friend and neighbor, Mr. Doug Harmon. Charles and Casey are about the same age and were already friends; they played baseball together when growing up. Casey had always wanted to make his living by farming, and working at Hatcher Family Dairy gave him a chance to do that. Casey had experience landscaping, farming, and fencing—Brimmage Tomlin would approve—before becoming a key member of our team and putting all his skills to good use.

Younger brother Cameron possessed experience in lawn maintenance and stall cleaning. Since coming to Hatcher Family Dairy, Cameron has become key milker and chief of the grounds crew for both farms. Both Harmon boys have mild dispositions, genuine smiles, and are pleasant to work with and be around.

Young Davo stopped by the vet clinic several years ago looking for work after recently moving from California. Jennifer gave him a chance and hired him to work at the clinic. Since then, Davo has worked many hours at the clinic and farm while attending college in preparation for becoming a veterinarian. I didn't realize there are rednecks in California, but Davo is living proof that there are some. When he arrived, Davo knew how to hunt and fish and had some agriculture knowledge acquired while working at a feed store in northern California. Davo is polite, respectful, and a quick learner with strength in technology. California redneck or not, he has become our go-to guy for all computer stuff at the farm and vet clinic as well as for the handling of livestock.

A resume from a military veteran had lain unnoticed in the creamery office for two weeks when Charles brought it to my attention. The resume was for Brian, an eleven-year Special Forces veteran and Bronze star recipient with absolutely no farm experience. I was so intrigued by his resume that I checked two of his references as soon as I could. One said, "He is an American patriot." The other said, "He is a first round draft pick." I hired him the next day.

His motivation for working for us was to gain enough farm experience to someday manage his own farm. On his first day of work, Brian showed up with a notebook and took notes all day long. He was well-organized, calculating, and cool under pressure. I knew we had a winner. Although short in stature, Brian appeared physically as though he could bench press and squat a whole lot of weight. He was equally good with his hands in combat and in woodworking. Brian carefully made an American and Tennessee flag from reclaimed wood crates for us to display for farm tours. We hung it in the barn loft next to the milk barn.

Brian took over one of the milk delivery routes, started milking the cows, fed the calves, took care of the chickens, and learned fencing from Casey. Within a short period of time, he was ready to manage his own farm. Family circumstances required Brian to move in order to manage his wife's family farm. Duty called and he answered. His dream to farm on his own came true. His short time here renewed my patriotism and has given me a better understanding of the great sacrifices these young military men and women make for this country. They command our respect.

All of these hard-working young men are *Farm Strong*; the Brimmage Tomlin's work-ethic mentality is scarce these days in modern society, but it is alive and well at Hatcher Family Dairy.

Chapter Twenty

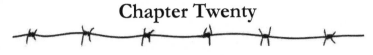

The Reality TV Show

Lucy had forwarded me an e-mail from a casting company looking for parents with good parenting skills to be on a reality television show dealing with troubled teenagers. I scanned over the e-mail and promptly dismissed it, thinking there was no way that they would be interested in Sharon and me for the show.

A few weeks later, Lucy asked me if I had responded to the e-mail and I said no, I had not. She convinced me to call the cell phone number on the e-mail just to see if they might be interested. I called the number and left a message since there was no answer. I simply said, "We are the Hatchers outside of Nashville, Tennessee. We live on a family dairy, beef, and sheep farm and bottle our own milk." Within five minutes someone from California called me right back. They wanted to come to the farm by the upcoming weekend to do some test filming.

Two Californians, a producer and a camera man, appeared at the farm a few days later to interview Sharon and me and get a feel for the farm. They liked what they saw. Ten days later, a temporary production trailer with all necessary equipment for the filming of a reality TV show was set up just outside the milk barn. A crew of twelve to fifteen was on the farm in preparation a week ahead of the actual filming.

Our house was converted into a studio with the addition of special lighting. Surveillance cameras were everywhere. The premise of the show was to have two troubled teens live with parents possessing good parenting skills for one week and film the impact of the stay or lack thereof on the teens and the host family.

The two teens, one boy and one girl, both sixteen years of age, were delivered to the farm from the airport around nine o'clock one Monday morning. Sharon promptly gave them their own coveralls and rubber boots. The rules of the household and farm were laid out to them. I told them both that the number one rule was not to mess with Sharon, and rule two was to refer to rule one.

For the next five days, twenty-four hours a day, these kids were our kids. They did everything we did for that entire week, including all farming activities. The kids got up early in the morning when we did—more accurately, we woke them up— and they retired in the evening by 10:00 p.m. as we did. No persuasion was required to put them to bed. All of us were completely exhausted by the end of the day.

The day's activities were filled mostly with duties that somebody on the farm had to perform every day anyway. Nothing was made up. The kids milked cows, cleaned the calf pens, fed the calves, stacked hay, hauled bottled milk, and fixed downed fences. At one point, our kids-for-a-week stole Sharon's *Ford 350* 4x4 farm truck in a desperate attempt to escape from the farm life that they thought was pure hell.

It was apparent the kids were not accustomed to hard work and had not worked a day in their lives. Sharon and the producer frantically stopped the farm truck just before they could get on the entry ramp for Interstate 840. Sharon told the teens that the truck was her property; they were not to drive it without her permission. The boy's only response was that he could buy our farm with the sale of his designer blue jeans. It was apparent to me that he put material things first in his life and had no appreciation whatsoever of what it means to live on a working farm.

Even though I had warned them, the kids had broken rule

one and rule two: Don't mess with Sharon. Sharon was livid. I had only seen her that angry a few times since we had been married, and I was scared. As their punishment, the two shoveled out a massive amount of cow manure from the milk-cow holding pen in a cold, light rain. Cleaning the holding pen is one of the hardest and dirtiest jobs on the whole farm.

The most humorous scene of the show was when the boy got some of the cow manure in his mouth while shoveling it. He exclaimed, "I got it in my mouth!" Sharon casually replied, "Wipe it on your sleeve." To their credit, their cleaning job of the holding pen was good. It took them about three and half hours to complete the task, but they did it.

Sharon and the girl had some serious altercations related to the girl's smoking habits. The house rules are no smoking. Cigarettes were found in the girl's loft. Sharon disposed of the cigarettes by tearing them apart and tossing the bits into the manure lagoon. The girl went into a fit of rage to the point that she aggressively cursed Sharon, using words rarely if ever spoken on the farm. Charles and Jennifer witnessed the girl's cussing fit and stood in total amazement of what had just occurred. I knew what they were thinking. If they had ever done that, Sharon would have backhanded them to the ground. I was in a total state of disbelief and wondered what I had gotten us into.

From that day forward, things began to improve. Sharon and the girl in a tearful reconciliation both apologized to each other, thus forming a strong bond between the two. I think the girl realized Sharon genuinely cared for her and that's why she wanted her to quit smoking. Discipline may have been one thing lacking in the lives of our temporary kids at their real homes, but they were responding favorably to it at the farm.

The next day, I planned on taking the young man up on the hill with me to repair a fence that a downed tree had broken. I contemplated what I would say to him to try to impact his life for the better. During the filming of the show, I had been reading the spiritual bestseller *The Shack*. To me, it was obvious that the most important thing in one's life is spiritual wellbeing. That's what I wanted to try to convey to him. I asked him, "What's most important in life?"

He responded, "Spending time with family and friends in a shopping mall."

I snapped back, "You have got to be kidding me! It's not material things—get that out of your mind. The most important thing is your spiritual side. The best part of my day is getting the cows up very early in the morning to be milked; the sun's coming up, the green pastures are surrounding me—that's when I make that spiritual connection."

Then the young man responded, rather perplexed, "Who are you connecting with?"

I quickly replied, "God, that's who!" and pointed up.

I still didn't think he grasped what I was saying. We finished the fence repair. I suggested we look for a four-leaf clover in the pasture field before we went back to the house for good luck. Within seconds, we did better than that: I found a seven-leaf clover. What are the chances of that? The boy realized this was something very special.

When we got back to the house, we went up to Charles's loft where the young man was staying. He wanted to put the seven-leaf clover in the Bible he brought with him during his stay for safe keeping. He admitted that the only reason he brought the Bible was that if we were a religious family, the Bible might impress us. I read Psalm 23 out loud to him in hopes that maybe he would realize that money, fancy jeans, and shopping junkets are *not* the most important thing in life. I think at that brief moment, perhaps he knew why I found comfort in that particular scripture; whether he will ever find comfort in Psalm 23 remains to be seen.

Sharon's relationship with the teenage girl while on the

farm seemed to have impacted both their lives. Sharon showed to me a real vulnerability that I had never seen in her before, a true tenderness. She really cared what happened in the girl's life, and the girl knew it. When the girl returned home, her grades dramatically improved. She even told her mother on the exit interview that the thing that she enjoyed most about her stay on the farm was that we did everything together as a family. She wanted so much to spend more time with her mother. Sharon and I both fought back tears.

There was an outpouring of emotional requests from parents all over the United States wanting to send their kids to the farm. They thought if only they could send their kids to spend some time with us, we could fix them. Why did they want to send their kids to the farm? Was it the farm itself or the work ethic? Or the family structure, or the discipline? Or the animals, or the time spent with the kids? Just what was it that made them think we could repair their child's behavior that had taken years to shape?

I was astonished to learn how many hurting kids there are all over America. Our hearts go out to them. For many of these kids, all they need is someone that cares enough to love them, spend time with them, teach them how to be responsible, and show them that God loves them, too. A farm is a good place to do all of this.

Time will tell whether we had any long term effect on these kids, but I doubt that they will soon forget the week that they spent with the Hatchers on the farm. One thing is for sure, America saw something it liked on Hatcher Family Dairy and wanted more of it. We had numerous offers to do similar reality shows, but Sharon said no, too much stress, disruption, and liability.

The Today Show

My wife Sharon never ceases to amaze me. I had gotten home from work one Wednesday late afternoon when she said to me, "You aren't going to believe what happened today."

I replied, "What?"

Sharon responded, "I entered the *Wake Up with Al Roker* competition by email at mid-morning today; by 1:30 p.m., NBC had emailed back that they want more information, photos, and video of the farm."

Sharon had been watching *The Today Show* that morning, jotted some ideas as to why Al should wake up on the farm, and my son Charles had crafted and sent a response email.

I stood for a moment in disbelief, and then asked, "You are kidding?"

Sharon wasn't kidding. The next day NBC wanted a video of Sharon inviting Al Roker to wake up on the farm. I took a short video of Sharon's invitation to Al by the front pond with the calves and chickens in the background. The gist of the invitation was: what better place to wake up with Al than on our farm? After all, Al could gather eggs and milk the cows himself to provide the freshest, best ingredients for as good a country breakfast as could be found anywhere.

I sent Sharon's video to NBC Friday morning. Things progressed quickly from that point. Late Monday evening, NBC called Sharon on her cell phone. She had been selected as one of the three finalists for the *Wake Up with Al* competition. The question that followed was: could she come to New York City for the announcement of the winner, live on *The Today Show*?

Sharon's initial response was yes, but she wanted other family members to go with her. Jennifer wanted to go and so did I. NBC agreed to pay our flights and cover our accommodations while in New York City. The Hatchers were going to New York City to be on national television. I couldn't help but think that our trip to the city would be much like the Clampetts from the *Beverly Hillbillies* going to Hollywood.

A limo driver met us at the airport with a sign that simply read *Hatchers*. The black SUV limo took us to the Manhattan Hotel, which is an upscale hotel not far from Rockefeller Plaza, the outdoor home of the *Today Show*. We were greeted by endless buildings reaching toward the sky. I'm much more comfortable looking up at the towering oak and maple trees next to the everlasting spring on the farm than at skyscrapers in the Big Apple.

We checked in to the hotel. The room had a modernist feel to it. The producer had told Sharon that she would have about forty-five seconds on live TV the next day to plead her case to Al, telling him why Al should wake up on the farm. Jennifer and I begin to put together the key message that would fit the time slot. Sharon practiced that forty-five second message over and over for some time, with Jennifer and me as her audience, until we all realized we were terribly hungry. The hotel desk recommended a reputable Italian restaurant within walking distance. Our experience at the restaurant was unforgettable.

The genuine Italian food and drink—from the pasta, wine, and bread to the dessert—was divine. We had convinced ourselves that there were several Mafia members dining around us and were somewhat intimidated. Soon, though, we realized that three rednecks from Tennessee posed no threat to an imaginary crime family in New York City.

I took photos of our meal to send back to the Hatchers left behind in Tennessee—doing the never-ending farm work—as proof of our fine dining. If there is one thing Hatchers like to do, it is to eat good food. The relentless practice with Sharon continued back at the hotel room until we couldn't stand it any longer. It was 2:00 a.m. when we finished. All of us were exhausted.

The limo picked us up the next morning at 5:00 a.m. in front of the hotel. We had to be at the studio at 6:00 that morning. A guard greeted us on the street at a side entrance. Our names were on a clipboard he held in his hand. He allowed us entrance into the building and instructed us to go down the hall to a second checkpoint and then a third, eventually arriving at the green room—the holding area—located on the second floor. A female guard was monitoring all those that entered the green room.

We brought with us freshly-churned Hatcher butter, carefully wrapped in freezer paper, along with a couple pints of chocolate milk and cream as gifts for Al and others on *The Today Show*. I wanted them to appreciate the fresh dairy products from the farm that we are able to enjoy every day. I placed the gifts in the small refrigerator in the green room and told one of the producers to make sure that Al at least got a taste of the butter. I never found out whether he ever got to enjoy the butter or not.

One big-screen TV hung on the wall with *The Today Show* airing live for those in the room to watch. A variety of fruit, cheese, and healthy snacks were available for the taking. I browsed on the food while Jennifer and Sharon were taken to the hair and makeup area in an adjacent room. I could see Sharon and Jennifer through the door as a hairdresser and makeup artist frantically worked on them for a good twenty minutes. They never looked better than when they emerged back to the green room, hair and makeup perfect.

On the other hand, when my turn came with no hair, the whole process took five minutes from start to finish. The makeup artist's biggest challenge was preventing glare from reflecting off my bald head. The end result, however, was much different than with Jennifer and Sharon. I didn't look any better with makeup on than before they started working on me.

Because I'm generally oblivious to my surroundings at times, Jennifer and Sharon had to inconspicuously point out to me famous people that happened to be in the green room with us. The redneck Hatchers mingled with celebrities ranging from sitcom and daytime drama actors to reality show stars.

The time came for our portion of the show. The three of us were led to the *Wake Up with Al* set on a raised platform outside in Rockefeller Plaza. Sharon, Jennifer and I sat in three chairs by ourselves with a noticeable lone empty chair to our right, presumably for Al. We sat there for what seemed like fifteen or twenty minutes until Al appeared, making his way to the empty chair.

The crowd that had lined the perimeters of the set began to wave and scream. Several large security guards held the crowd back. Time seemed to stand still. The clouds in the sky, the people, and the entire *Wake Up with Al* set froze. At that moment I looked straight up at the skyscrapers and wondered, "*Is this really happening? How in the world did we get on national television?*" Were we going to come across as Tennessee hillbillies or perhaps the biggest rednecks the world had ever seen?

Time started flowing normally again. Al sat down in the empty chair. Before the cameras started rolling, Al put us at ease instantly with his smile and genuine demeanor. I could just feel that this was going to be a good experience.

Sharon never got the opportunity to use the forty-five-second pitch that she had worked so hard on. Al mainly talked to Sharon about the farm. Jennifer and I didn't have to say much, just agree with the conversation. We exited the platform for the other two finalists to take their turns before the winner was to be announced.

The three finalists were brought back out on to the set with their friends and family. Al announced that the winner would be the one with an alarm clock under the box in front of them. On

Al's signal, each finalist raised their box. There was an alarm clock under each box. The finalists were not finalists at all, we were all winners. Al was going to each winner's location to broadcast *Wake Up with Al*. The *Today Show* was going to Hatcher Family Dairy first, in one week. I was in shock. It was all due to Sharon's efforts. This was another reminder to me just how truly special Sharon is.

**The *Today Show* at Rockefeller Plaza in New York City.
Al Roker, Sharon, Jennifer, and myself.**

We—the Hatchers—enjoyed our time in New York City, but we were somewhat intimidated by the crowds of people, the towering buildings, the subway, all the bright lights, and the rapid pace of life. We realized that we do live in a vacuum on the farm in a simpler kind of world, but we wouldn't have it any other way. Only minutes from Brentwood, Tennessee—one of the highest income-per-capita areas in the United States—the farm acts as a sanctuary, protecting us from present-day urban life and all that goes with it.

The Today Show was coming to the farm the following Wednesday. Sharon was in a full panic, realizing she had only a few days of preparation before the arrival of *The Today Show* and, for all practical purposes, the whole world. To make matters worse, I was at a State Animal Health Official's meeting in Arkansas while most of the farm preparation work was taking place. As I was driving back from the meeting, I thought about what was about to occur the next day. I knew that people from across the country would get a glimpse of the Hatchers in our true setting, on the farm.

My biggest concern was whether we could portray the American farm family and agriculture appropriately. All we had to do was to be transparent, show the passion we have for taking care of the animals and land, and be ourselves. I felt like we could do that. We would know the answer to that question soon. I arrived back home Tuesday evening at about 7 p.m., just hours before *The Today Show* was to arrive. Sharon was as I had left her, still in panic mode. All of us continued to make preparations until midnight or after. As usual, Sharon was still working when I went to bed and was also the first one up the next morning.

Jennifer and Chuck came down off the hill from their house around 2:15 in the morning. They could see bright lights coming from the milk barn area as they approached. Jennifer said the area was lit up like the Nashville airport or Times Square—we had just seen Times Square a week earlier. The crew and several satellite trucks were already set up. Al magically appeared around 2:30 in the morning. From 2:30 a.m. to 4:00 a.m., Al did some segments for *The Weather Channel* as well as for our local NBC affiliate in the calf area with the holding pen in the background.

Charles brought the cows down off the hill at 4:00 in the morning. The cows were already confused because Charles woke them early. The bright lights and the strangers about just added to their confusion. I imagine the cows were feeling a bit out of place just as we were a week earlier in New York City.

**Al Roker in the calf nursery area during the filming of the
Today Show weather segments on the farm.**

Charles gave Al a short course on how to milk the cows.
The crew had purchased some coveralls for Al to protect him
from the potential blasts of cow manure and urine during
milking, but they didn't fit. Sharon saved the day, as usual, by
providing Al with coveralls that did fit. On and off for the next
several hours, the crew filmed three-to-five-minute segments of
Al doing the weather and performing some of the farm
activities. Al got to feed the baby calves bottles of milk—this
was the funniest part since one of the calves almost knocked
the bottle out of Al's hands. Al milked some of the cows.
When the sun came up, it was a beautiful day. The farm could
not have looked any better.

A scrumptious, heaping country breakfast had been
prepared by a local chef using our milk, cream, and eggs,
supplemented by local sausage, country ham, and jams. The
bountiful breakfast, along with overflowing plates of eggs,
biscuits and sausage gravy, was displayed on our kitchen table.
Jennifer, Chuck, Sharon, Charles, and I sat around our kitchen
table with Al showing the heaping breakfast dishes to the
television camera, but we didn't have time to eat any of them.

We were then beckoned outside for the final segment. It wasn't until after the filming was complete that we finally were able to fully enjoy the incredible breakfast. We are rarely accustomed to such a big breakfast. It was a real treat.

I knew we had accomplished our mission in portraying agriculture as we know, love, and live it when Al said, "Farmers are the backbone of America." He also said that farmers work hard every day to supply America with food. The entire crew and Al told us how much fun that they had had on the farm. I think Al had more fun than anyone. The very last thing Al did on camera was to drive the big *960 Ford* tractor pulling the wagon loaded with friends and family. He waved as he pulled away. The smile on his face told the story. Al was having the time of his life.

Something else good came from *The Today Show's* visit to the farm. A young man—a teenager, really—named Alex came to work for us and learned some valuable life lessons while he was on the farm. Al Roker and his wife are Alex's godparents. Because of Al's visit to our farm, Alex's parents wanted their son to experience farm life. Their wish came true. The summer following our appearance on *The Today Show*, the young teenager performed some of the most menial tasks on the farm. He cared for the bottle calves and chickens and also helped with the farm tours most of the hot summer. The caretaking of the chickens and calves can be the dirtiest, hottest, and hardest job on the farm because of the physical work required in removing the chicken manure from the laying coop and the calf manure from the baby-calf pens.

Much to our surprise, this city boy did a great job for us under trying conditions. He never complained and was very polite and courteous. The time he spent with us was mutually rewarding. The young man learned where food comes from while gaining an appreciation for hard physical labor and a job well done, just as I had learned those summers many years ago with Granddad. Many in today's world don't understand or appreciate where their food comes from. Alex was a big help to us while he was here, greatly decreasing our daily workload; now he knows where his food comes from, too.

Chapter Twenty-One

Old Man Winter

Dealing with the weather is an occupational hazard of being a farmer. The drought of 2012 had taught us about hot and dry. Now it was time for Old Man Winter to expose us to the other extreme: bitter cold. Early January 2014, the weather man had been predicting record cold weather for a week and we knew the farm had to be ready.

Preparations for the cold weather had begun two days prior to the predicted cold. Antifreeze levels on all vehicles, including the old blue pickup truck and all tractors, were checked, all exposed water pipes were covered, all water troughs were filled to the top, and any water hoses were disconnected, drained, and stored inside. The milk-cow and all heifer lot hay-rings were filled with hay. The two well houses and the one spring house were outfitted with small thermostat-controlled electric heaters.

Sharon purchased some tarps for me to install on the northwest end of the baby calf area to protect the calves from the wind. During extreme cold it is critical that livestock get extra forage and feed to supply energy for the body to combat the cold. And of course, humans and animals must have water. It's hard to supply livestock with water if the water supply is frozen.

The extreme cold was expected to move in late on a Sunday evening. After church on Sunday, we pulled all the tractors under cover in the big hay shed. The tractor engine warmers were plugged in on all three tractors to ensure that all would start when called upon to put out the necessary hay, silage, and feed to the cattle.

The temperature dropped fifty degrees Fahrenheit as the front moved in that afternoon and night. The farm was on high alert. All of us were nervously aware of what the consequences would be if our preparations failed. The immediate family—Sharon, myself, Jennifer, Chuck, Charles, Gabaga, and Parker—were all gathered at Gabaga and Parker's house for our usual Sunday evening family dinner on this very unusual night.

As we sat down at the dinner table to eat, we heard something pelting the living room windows, *clack, clack, clack*. Anxious to see what was going on outside, I stepped out the front door of the house onto the front sidewalk and looked down toward the hay shed's security light. Frozen precipitation, part snow, part sleet, and part freezing rain, could be seen flowing sideways in the dim winter night. In a matter of minutes, the ground and all the outside vehicles were covered with a shiny white frozen exterior.

One of our heavily pregnant cows in the dry lot was due to calve any day. If the calf was born on this night and had any chance of survival, the mother must give birth and lick her calf dry quickly, and the calf must nurse the mother's first rich yellow milk—colostrum—quickly. We all wondered whether our cold weather preparations were enough and were fearful of what the morning light would reveal. This was the first of three polar vortices—that's what the weatherman affectionately called these extreme cold blasts—the farm would endure throughout the month of January 2014.

The low the first night was supposed to be ten degrees Fahrenheit, but the weather man missed the mark. The strong winds drove the wind chill to well below zero. At daylight the next morning, the outside digital thermometer read 1.4° F. By the third day of the extreme cold, every water trough was frozen solid with three to four inches of thick ice on top. The expecting mother cow did calve on the second night of the first cold snap and did a spectacular job of taking care of her baby. The calf survived.

The painstaking task of breaking the ice on each and every trough and pond in every lot with an ax took three to four hours each time. Once the ice had formed and temperatures were below freezing, this routine had to be continued twice daily to keep the livestock watered.

The only front-end loader we have is mounted on the *Ford 9600* tractor, which has no cab to protect the driver from the frigid elements. All livestock were fed extra hay, silage, and feed during the periods of extreme cold to supply the increased energy necessary to maintain body heat. Charles was the lucky individual that got to do most of the tractor work during the three Arctic blast periods.

All the daily chores during the extreme cold periods took twice as long as normal because of having to break the ice, supply extra feed, and go through all the steps necessary to keep the water pipes from freezing. It was absolutely imperative to us that all the animals had plenty of food and water.

During much of the cold weather, my brother Jim was recovering from hernia surgery and couldn't lift more than ten pounds for over a month. Charles' main responsibility on Wednesdays is to make sure our milk is delivered to our retail customers. Although Charles took the brunt of the extra work, I milked the cows every Wednesday morning for some time, covering Jim's milking shift and work for that day while he recovered.

Any time the nightly temperature dropped into the teens or below—and that was often during the winter of 2014—the milk barn had to be put through a cold-night protocol to prevent water and milking equipment from freezing. We would securely fasten all doors to prevent the cold air from coming in.

We would fill up and plug in the large, torpedo, forced-air diesel heater because it had to run all night to keep things warm in the milking parlor. The feed room door would also need to be propped open so that the warm air could penetrate the room and keep the water pipes that passed through the feed room into the milking parlor from freezing.

**Livestock watering trough on the hill
during the arctic blast.**

Even though we did this correctly each night, the hot-water supply pipe still froze and burst twice during the marathon cold period. That wasn't the only problem we had, either: during one evening milking, the vacuum pump froze up even though it was being warmed by two heaters. The pump seizing up caused the belts to be chewed up and spit off by the pulleys. Milking was delayed for two hours while the vacuum pump thawed out and new belts could be obtained from a late-night auto parts store. It was 10 p.m. that night before milking was complete.

The night before I subbed for Jim's Wednesday morning milking and daily chores, Charles gave me some good advice, "Make sure the milk barn is ready for the cold weather tonight, and when you are on the tractor tomorrow, you better put something over your face or the cold air will burn it." I took his advice and double-checked the milk barn to see if the cold-weather prep had been done, and it had.

When the alarm went off the next morning at 4:45 a.m., I sat on the edge of the bed for a few minutes contemplating what my day was going to be like. When my feet hit the cold hardwood floor, a chill went up my spine. I knew on this frigid morning my best chance of staying warm while working outside was to dress in layers. I pulled up my blue jeans, sat back down on the edge of the bed to put on my insulated boot socks, then stretched a thermal shirt over my t-shirt and followed it with a long-sleeve, button-up flannel shirt.

I made my way into the kitchen to make myself a cup of coffee with hot frothy milk to warm myself up and wake up. I was curious to see if the temperature had made it down to zero. Not quite but almost. The outside temperature digital thermometer read 1.4° F again for the second time this winter. The wind chill was well below zero.

My outer winter clothing of choice is *Carhartt* clothing because it's resistant to the hazards of barb wire and heavily insulated to protect against the elements. I like to wear *Carhartt* insulated bib coveralls over my blue jeans so that I can remove my heavy *Carhartt* outer jacket if needed, freeing my arms up to artificially breed a cow. Donning my *Carhartt* gear and heavy outer jacket with hood, I snapped the furry, flapped hat securely below my chin—the same type of flying-squirrel hat that Mr. Tomlin wore—put on insulated leather gloves and high top insulated *Muck* boots, and finally stepped out into the cold darkness.

I could hear the wind howling through the hall of the barn.

Much to my amazement, after turning the barn lights on to assess any damage from freezing, I saw that neither the water nor the vacuum pump was frozen. The milking system went through the pre-milking sanitizing cycle uneventfully. Our preparations had paid off.

A few cows had made their way to the holding pen. Warm cow manure and urine hit the frigid concrete, creating clouds of billowing steam and lowering visibility so that I couldn't see the back gate of the holding pen. Web-like white icicles hung from the hair surrounding the cows' nostrils, created by the warm exhaled air as it met the cold external air. Any cow manure or urine that hit the concrete immediately froze. The ground was frozen solid, too, turning the farm into frozen tundra.

As I gathered the rest of the cows up for milking, I noticed that except for the wind, there was an eerie silence. The usual sloshing noises the cows and I normally made when walking off the hill in the mud were absent. We were walking on a subzero, frozen surface as hard as concrete.

It took an hour or more each time to milk the cows because of all the extra steps necessary during the extreme cold. We had to open and close the milk cows' entrance and exit to the milking parlor for each set of cows milked in order to retain the warmth inside the barn. The cows themselves, along with the diesel-powered, forced-air heater, generated enough heat in the milking parlor to keep the temperature above freezing.

I breathed a sigh of relief when the last cow exited the milking parlor. After spraying out the area, I struggled to shut the exterior doors of the barn because of the ice buildup from repeated washings. Finally, my morning milking was complete; it was now midmorning and I hadn't put out hay yet for the milk cows and all the heifer lots. I had the unenviable task of climbing aboard the unheated cab-less tractor to deliver the hay.

Since I was already bundled up and it would take me a

considerable amount of time to disrobe and re-dress with additional extreme weather attire, I decided to delay my breakfast until I finished the tractor work. I remembered what Charles had said about protecting my face if I rode the tractor. Finding no face mask, I improvised by fashioning one out of a red bandanna, pulling it over my nose and tying it at the back of my neck, then replacing my furry ear-flap hat and pulling my *Carhartt* jacket hood over my head. The only exposed areas of my face were my eyes and the area around them. I looked like someone from the Wild West ready to rob a bank.

I unplugged the engine heater of the big *9600 Ford* tractor, climbed up and mounted the tractor seat, started the engine, and headed uphill along the driveway. The stinging cold penetrated the red bandana onto my face, but it was tolerable. However, the cold was burning my eyes. I thought to myself that maybe I should have worn eye protection, too. Warm tears began to stream down my cheeks in a stinging path.

I was greeted in several paddocks by heifers running and buck-jumping in excitement over the arrival of the new hay. They didn't seem to mind the cold weather at all. Despite my best efforts, I, on the other hand, was chilled to the bone when I arrived back at the house after delivering hay. My hands and feet were beginning to get numb and the exposed skin areas around my eyes were on fire.

Luckily, Sharon had a roaring fire going in the fireplace, so I was able to thaw out while sipping hot coffee with frothed whole milk from my *Nespresso* machine. The next day, the area on my face around my eyes not protected by the bandana was fire-engine red, resembling the mask of a raccoon, only red instead of black.

All of us on the farm were beginning to feel like we did during the drought of 2012, wondering when these dreadful weather conditions would end. The same cold weather procedures were being performed day after day after day with no end in sight. The cows had to be milked and the livestock watered and fed regardless of the weather conditions.

The winter weather continued through February and into March. On March 3, 2014, Old Man Winter blasted us with some more freezing rain. We always keep our fingers crossed when freezing rain is predicted for fear of losing electrical power as we did in 1994. The farm didn't lose electricity on this day, but I witnessed an amazing sight as a result of the freezing rain while I was gathering the cows for milking.

My son Charles had installed a fenced cow path—a sort of road or lane—up the steepest part of the hill the previous fall so that the milk cows could access the pasture lots on top of the hill during the winter without making a muddy mess. The project was just one of a series of improvements in our farm conservation efforts.

An isolated area in the cow lane on the steepest part of the cow lane had become as slick as glass with a coating of black ice. One of our most docile, unexcitable Jersey cows walked onto the slick spot and began to slide down the hill. The cow remained upright, never lost her footing, and ice skated to the bottom of the hill, picking up speed as she went past a dozen cows as she descended. She reached the bottom of the hill and looked back at me as if to ask, "Did you see that?"

I hadn't seen a better performance from an Olympic speed skater. The cow continued on to the milk barn like nothing ever happened. That was the last day of winter-like conditions before the spring of 2014. The farm had experienced a flood, extreme drought, heat, and cold in a span of four years, and had survived.

Chapter Twenty-two

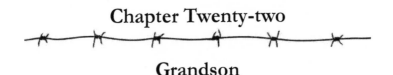

Grandson

I have never been known for keeping secrets. Sharon and Charles say that I can't keep a secret to save my soul. The ultimate test of my secret-keeping abilities was about to occur. I was going to prove to them that I could keep a secret and a big one at that.

Throughout Jennifer's whole life, she was mature beyond her years. Boys were not a priority for her because she was always focused on becoming a veterinarian. Even as a teenager, Jennifer never really had a serious boyfriend. As she approached thirty years of age, Sharon and I wondered whether she would ever get married and if we would ever have grandkids.

Before my mother-in-law, Gabaga, retired, she worked at the Ellington Agricultural campus for the Tennessee Wildlife Resources Agency. This is the same campus that houses the Tennessee Department of Agriculture where I work. Once, while Jennifer was visiting Gabaga at work, she caught the eye of an astute wildlife officer who happened to be at the office that day. The officer's name was Chuck.

Chuck is a tall, slender, moderately-muscled young man with chiseled facial features. On occasion Chuck flashes a beaming smile, exposing his nearly-perfect white teeth. Many say he resembles the well-liked *NASCAR* race-car driver Carl Edwards. Chuck was so enamored with Jennifer that he asked Gabaga who in the world she was. Gabaga responded by saying, "Why, that's my granddaughter!"

The poor young man tried on a number of occasions to make contact with Jennifer, only to be snubbed by her each time. Jennifer was reluctant to become involved in a relationship—even at that point in her life. I had warned Jennifer early in life about the way that men can be. She had never forgotten what I told her. To his credit, Chuck persisted. He realized what a find Jennifer was. Finally, one day Jennifer confided in Sharon about the wildlife officer's interest in her. She asked Sharon what to do about his persistence. Sharon said, "Just go out with him. You don't have to marry him." Little did Sharon know that Jennifer would, a few months later, marry Chuck.

Sharon's motherly advice was the gentle stimulus needed for Jennifer to initiate a courtship with Chuck. Still uncertain and cautious, she agreed to meet Chuck at a crowded restaurant in broad daylight, just to be safe in case he turned out to be a mass murderer. After a few weeks of courtship, Chuck was coming around the farm more and more. It was obvious to me, even as oblivious as I tend to be, that the two were madly in love.

Chuck approached me one day at the milk store while I was unloading milk. He was visibly nervous as he began to speak. I thought I knew what he was about to say and my heart pounded in anticipation. Chuck's face paled when he said, "Dr. Hatcher, I would like to marry your daughter and I would much appreciate your permission."

I was not surprised at all by his request but was still stunned, realizing I was going to lose my little girl, my only daughter, to a man. I did approve Chuck's request. Chuck asked that I not divulge the subject of our conversation until he could purchase an engagement ring and pop the question to Jennifer. Even though I was dying to tell someone about this important news, I told no one, not even Sharon.

The few days that followed seemed like an eternity. When

Chuck finally told me that I could reveal the secret, I spilled my guts to Sharon and Charles. They told me it was the only secret I had ever kept in my life.

A few weeks later, Jennifer and Chuck were married in a small, private family ceremony at the same exact location that my granddad and grandmother camped out on, above the everlasting spring, during that summer so many years ago. The wedding took place amidst the intensely green wheat and crimson red clover pasture on a beautiful sunny day early in spring. The birds of the field were singing triumphantly through the ceremony, and a majestic blue sky arched above us.

Four years later, son-in-law Chuck placed a bottle of fine ten-year-old whiskey on our dining room table with two shot glasses. He began to pour the whiskey into each glass as he said, "I told you I wasn't going to open this bottle of whiskey until something special has happened and it has. Jennifer is pregnant."

Sharon is usually the first to know about family matters. I am usually the last to know, as I am seemingly oblivious to many things. This is common knowledge to those that know me. Regardless, I was tickled to death to hear the news. I had wanted a baby for many years but never could talk Sharon into adopting or having a third child. This was perfect, though—a grandbaby was on the way, and I was in heaven.

A few months later, Jennifer had purchased a state-of-the-art ultrasound machine and, as any good veterinarian would do, ultra-sounded herself. Jennifer was convinced the baby was a boy and insisted that I confirm. Sure enough, when I held the ultrasound probe at just the right spot, the male genitalia flashed like a beacon in the night on the screen. A month later, Jennifer's doctor confirmed our diagnosis. It was now time to select a name. Jennifer and Chuck had considered all sorts of names and combinations of names before Chuck insisted on Hatcher being the first name. The Hatcher name was that important to him.

Jennifer had actually kept her last name of Hatcher when she and Chuck married. When they told me that the first name of my grandson would be Hatcher, in my exuberance, I blurted out, "Hatcher Hatcher, I like that." I had completely forgotten that my grandson's last name would be Yoest.

Even during her pregnancy, Jennifer was active on the farm. For over an hour, Jennifer (seven months pregnant), Chuck, all the dogs (B, Gator, Betsy and Jane) and I had been trying to move the seven market lambs in the L-shaped lot beside the veterinary clinic to the small lot right above it. My lower back was hurting, making me that much more easily irritated. We needed to move the sheep so that a new group of recently-weaned dairy heifers could occupy the lot. We had tried everything to move the sheep out of the lot: coercing them out with feed, slowly and calmly driving them out, and then not so calmly running them out. After repeated attempts, three of the seven darted through the gate, but the other four idiots would not go near it. They dashed wildly around with their heads high in reckless abandonment, jumping gleefully in the air as if they were Santa's reindeer.

I told Chuck that if I had a gun, shooting them and field dressing them right then and there would be a good option. We made one last desperate attempt to run the remaining defiant sheep out of the lot, but just as we got them to the gate, Betsy, Gator, and Jane barked, causing the sheep to go in the opposite direction. At that point, Chuck lost his temper too and scolded the dogs severely. That's when Jennifer—the only calm one of all those involved—suggested that we have Sharon give it a try before someone or some sheep got hurt, especially since it was about the time of day Sharon fed them anyhow. I was fine with that.

I went back down to the house to request Sharon's assistance. She agreed to help and then methodically, as she does every day, loaded the sheep feed and hay into the back of the little red *Chevrolet S10* pickup truck, drove up to the clinic, opened the gate to the lot, called the sheep in a soothing voice, and placed the feed and hay in the trough in the makeshift corral. The sheep walked right into the corral and began to eat, and Sharon shut the corral gate.

In total amazement, I witnessed the whole thing from the house driveway some three hundred yards away. Wasn't this the same thing Jennifer, Chuck, the dogs, and I had tried to do for much of the afternoon—and Sharon does it in thirty seconds? What was the difference? I realized that the difference was Sharon. Sharon is the shepherd to the sheep. The idiot sheep recognized the familiar, protective voice and scent of Sharon and were immediately at ease. The sheep trusted her and would follow her anywhere.

All the references in the Bible to Jesus as the Good Shepherd make perfect sense to me in light of this experience. I'm sure God sometimes views us as idiots, too, when we are high-headed like the uncooperative sheep. Psalm 23, my favorite scripture, says that "the Lord is my shepherd...his rod and his staff they comfort me;" those words carry even more meaning now because of this and many other farm experiences.

I'm a step slower, not as strong, and a few pounds heavier than I was when catching goats for Granddad so many years ago. The sheep reminded me of this again recently. Jennifer and I were sorting ewes in the hallway of the sheep barn one day in preparation for doing ultrasounds to see if they are pregnant. Sheep are generally submissive once they are caught, but the initial catching is often challenging. After one or two failed attempts to grab a certain ewe, I reached out with my right arm to grab a ewe as she approached me at full speed. In an attempt to avoid capture, she jumped directly onto my awaiting arm. A stinging sensation like an electrical shock shot up the inside of my arm. I looked down to see my bicep muscle roll up slowly from its distal attachment to just below the inside of my shoulder in an ugly ball. I knew instantly what I had done. I had torn my bicep tendon and muscle. The big, fat, escaped ewe glanced back at me as to say, "Ha, ha, who's the dummy now!"

We had Dr. Sam's (Jennifer's associate) wedding to go to later that Saturday afternoon. I knew that my condition was not an emergency and that I had plenty of time to consult with a surgeon to schedule a repair. I could wait until Monday to do that. Much to Sharon's chagrin, I fashioned a sling from remnants of materials kept from previous injuries to protect my arm and we headed to the wedding a few hours later.

My torn biceps tendon was fully repaired the next week. After several weeks of physical therapy and the avoidance of heavy use of the biceps muscle, I'm as good as new.

Lesson learned from the sheep: don't try to catch a heavy ewe running full speed by you. Since then, I have purchased a $3000 sheep-handling chute.

Hatcher's birth

Jennifer called the house Saturday morning on March 15, 2014, at 7:00 a.m. She had been having some sporadic abdominal contractions since 2:00 a.m. The excitement for the arrival of our first grandchild had been building all week. Jennifer worked at the vet clinic during the entire pregnancy, performing all duties except those that might expose her to the damaging direct kick of a cow or horse, essentially until the time of delivery. It had only been in the last several weeks that Jennifer had slowed down some, having to take periodic breaks to rest in a reclining chair between vet exams. I hadn't seen her sit still since she was a baby.

The full name of my grandson was going to be Hatcher Abram Yoest. His initials are HAY. The middle name, Abram, was after my father, Abram Wooldridge Hatcher, and my great-grandfather, Abram Wooldridge Hatcher. Hatcher Abram Yoest would be the sixth generation of Abram Hatcher's direct descendants to live on this same farm. I knew that Hatcher would have the same opportunities I had to be shaped and molded by this farm. I was extremely thankful, believing firmly that there is no better place than a farm to raise children. Many say that there is nothing like being a grandparent. I would soon find out if this is true. The significance of this birth event was beginning to sink in. I became increasingly emotional as the time for delivery drew closer, not only because of the importance of the continued heritage, but also because I would become a grandfather for the first time.

Jennifer and Chuck left for the hospital around 8:00 a.m. as the contractions were beginning to become more frequent. It was our first beautiful, spring-like, sunny day since the harsh winter. I decided that my dog B and I had plenty of time to take a walk on the farm until we heard back from Jennifer after the doctor had the chance to examine her.

B was oblivious to the upcoming birth of my grandson as he chased squirrels up the oak trees and geese around the pond with reckless abandonment. He ran in circles around the pond and abruptly dove in at one point, swimming for a while before returning to the pond bank at full speed. The birds were singing triumphantly in celebration of the spring day after a long, painfully cold winter—or maybe they just knew that Hatcher was coming.

The past winter had been the worst ever for winter

pasture. Ordinarily the cows can graze winter wheat and red clover in February, but that hadn't been the case this winter. This was the first week that there was enough growth of the wheat and clover for the cows to be rotated on to the winter pasture fields. The extraordinary winter which we had endured seemed to stop that morning. The cows had been granted access to the paddock on the south side of the farm next to our neighbors, the Harmons. Some of the cows were lying down, perfectly content with a belly full of fresh grass and chewing their cuds without a care in the world, while others were grazing as fast as possible until they too could become full.

A feeling of peace came over me as I soaked up my surroundings and just for a moment, I thought I could feel my dad's—Abram's—presence. Just then, my cell phone rang. It was Sharon, wanting to know where in the world I was and what I was doing. Her order was to get my butt down to the house. It was time to go to the hospital. B and I headed back to the house, both of us feeling better after taking a walk on the farm.

Sharon, Charles, and I got to the hospital around mid-morning. Chuck's family, including his parents, sisters, and in-laws, arrived a few hours after we did. Camp was set up in the family waiting room as we anxiously awaited Hatcher's birth. The country folk had come to the big city.

Throughout the day, Chuck, his dad, and I made regular trips to the local coffee shop. By late afternoon, I was getting hungry, running out of patience, and Jennifer wasn't making much progress. Some of us decided to make a dash to *Frothy Monkey*—one of our best coffee shop milk customers—to eat supper. When we returned to the hospital, Jennifer had progressed to the point that the doctor wanted to try to deliver Hatcher. The nurse ran all of us except Chuck out of the room.

Jennifer pushed hard for about thirty minutes until her blood pressure dropped, prompting the doctor to suspend the attempt. Jennifer's doctor and I talked for a while about the parallels of delivering babies versus calves and foals. I won't bore you with the details, but the procedures are all basically the same. I thought maybe the whole birthing process would be gentler with humans than with animals, but it is not. I told the doctor that I probably had delivered more calves, foals, puppies, and kittens than she had human babies, but she wasn't impressed. I'm fully convinced I could deliver a baby if needed, although I had no desire to assist with the birth of my grandson.

A second attempt for delivery was initiated a few hours later. We had heard no news from Chuck or the doctor about Jennifer's progress for what seemed an eternity, and eventually I couldn't stand not knowing any longer. I decided to leave the family waiting room to do a little reconnaissance of my own. The entrance to the birthing area was locked and guarded. Access was granted after I flashed the designated wristband at the camera. The attending nurse hit the button, releasing the locked door and giving me entrance.

I looked over at the nurse's station and down the hall. The coast was clear. I stealthily scampered down the hall, being careful to avoid detection and tiptoeing like the *Grinch*. I reached the outside of the birthing room door in the hallway when I heard Jennifer vocalizing almost rhythmically as she strained to push Hatcher out. The noises I heard were familiar to me. I recognized the pain and desperation in the moans of Jennifer. The mama cows at the hundreds of difficult calvings I attended as a veterinarian over the years sounded the same way during the throes of a difficult birth.

I could handle the delivery of baby animals, but this was different—this was my daughter. I was not comfortable with it. I left quickly, heading back to the family waiting room with my tail between my legs. My heart went out to Jennifer, hoping that this whole birthing process would come to an end soon. I thought to myself that this was the beginning of the many sacrifices that Jennifer would make for her son. I completely understood the powerful mother-child bond after witnessing what Jennifer was going through. Nonetheless, I felt terrible that my little girl was suffering like this.

When I got back to the waiting room, everyone wanted to know what I found out. I told them that Jennifer was in the midst of the birthing battle. A long fifteen minutes later, Chuck came to the entrance of the waiting room, appearing somewhat pale after taking in what just had occurred. He was relieved but excited at the same time. He proudly proclaimed, "He's here!" Hatcher was born around 11:20 p.m. The birthing process for Hatcher had taken nearly twenty-four hours.

Sitting in a chair in the birthing room, Chuck handed Hatcher to me. I carefully held him, making sure to support his head and neck. Looking down at the sixth generation Hatcher of College Grove, Tennessee, I wondered: what kind of personality will he have? Will he love the farm as much as I? Will I live to see him grow up to become a young man? Only God knows.

Jennifer, Chuck and Hatcher came home that following Monday to the same house that Sharon and I brought Jennifer home to nearly thirty-five years earlier. The house has been remodeled and expanded but remains far from extravagant. Even with all the development around the farm, Jennifer, Chuck, and Hatcher's closest non-Hatcher neighbor is nearly a mile away. The milk cows grazing in the green fields surrounding the house provide a certain solace like no other place on earth. My son Charles is right: our forefathers did walk the same footsteps as we do today. My first grandchild will be able to walk those same footsteps on the farm, too. I couldn't be happier.

Hatcher lived in misery the first six months of his life. Jennifer was unable to nurse, necessitating the use of formula.

Hatcher was colicky and regurgitated so much that the doctor thought he was allergic to milk—not really a diagnosis a dairy family wanted to hear. It was even mentioned that he might have an esophageal issue. The doctor prescribed some sort of hypoallergenic (non-milk) formula costing nearly a hundred dollars a can. I tasted the formula one day to see what Hatcher was experiencing. It tasted like burnt onions marinated in metal chips. I immediately spit the formula out of my mouth and got a little nauseated—poor Hatcher. After months of sleepless nights and Hatcher's sluggish growth rate (he lost weight for a while), out of desperation Chuck hatched a plan, and I was in on it. We decided not to tell Sharon and Jennifer for fear of immediate rejection and scolding. It was a simple plan. The plan was to slowly incorporate Hatcher whole milk into Hatcher's bottle until the formula was eliminated altogether.

A few days into the plan, as Hatcher consistently showed no ill effects from the gradual addition of the whole milk, Chuck had the courage to tell Sharon and Jennifer what he had done. They were a little upset with Chuck, but not much, since Hatcher was improving daily as his intestinal issues began to decrease. The whole milk was continued for several weeks after that, until the last can of the dreadful-tasting formula was used up. At Hatcher's next doctor's appointment, the results of the Hatcher whole-milk diet were readily apparent: Hatcher had gone from a dismal thirty-something percentile on the growth chart to a whopping ninety-eighth percentile. There was a baby boy in Nebraska that was larger. The doctor was very impressed; it caused him to rethink his previous opinion on the use of whole milk in babies.

Now at 27 months of age and over forty pounds, Hatcher is a curly-headed, toddler giant dynamo, strong as an ox and never still. We are not real sure where the curly hair comes from. The tightness of the coils of his golden locks is directly controlled by the ambient heat and humidity. People say there is nothing like having grandkids, and it's true. They say and do the darndest things. Hatcher runs to me in reckless abandonment (just like my dog B) and with great exuberance every time he sees me, launching himself into my awaiting arms. Jennifer has chosen to have him call me "doc" but he has difficulty in pronouncing "doc" and instead calls me "cock"— the term for a male chicken or rooster. This seems very cute until he blurts it out in church, which he has. It is a little hard to explain this to the preacher. After weeks of correction, he is beginning to say "doc" now.

My grandson, Hatcher Abram Yoest. His initials are HAY.

Hatcher greatly prefers being outdoors and loves riding tractors. He rides with me for hours strapped in the jump seat of the cabbed McCormick tractor. When his mother comes to get him, he cries. I believe now that he will be a farmer.

Hatcher acquired the nickname of Deags early on. The nickname came via a much loved little Yorkie dog we called "chigger" that passed away several years ago. Chigger's nickname was "little deagle." I called Hatcher a "precious little deagle" even before he was born. Little Deagle was later shortened to Deags, and that's what I call him today. When Hatcher acts up, I call him dirty Deags.

Hatcher is a very happy child most of the time, unless he doesn't get enough sleep. I have noticed he is happiest when he is surrounded by his family. It has become a tradition of ours that every Sunday evening, the four generations living on the farm gather to eat a fabulous, locally-derived supper together at Gabaga and Parker's house. The summer meals are the best, supplied by products produced on our farm (beef, milk, cream, and lamb) and fresh seasonal produce from my farmer friends at the farmers market. The typical fare might include fresh-cut, homegrown tomatoes with basil and mozzarella cheese; fried okra; green beans; corn on the cob; Gabaga's best-in-the-world potato salad; steaks; burgers; lamb chops; or roast; all finished up with homemade ice cream or fresh strawberry shortcake and Hatcher whipped cream.

Few people in the world eat as well as we do on Sunday nights. In attendance almost every Sunday are four generations, Gabaga and Parker (generation 1), Sharon and myself (generation 2), Chuck and Jennifer, Charles and his girlfriend, Mary, (generation 3), and Hatcher (generation 4). Hatcher takes great delight in calling the names of all those in attendance one by one. At the conclusion, he claps wildly while laughing out loud. We all join him in applause. I have never seen a person of any age derive such pure satisfaction from such a little thing.

Then I realized this isn't such a little thing at all; how many children are fortunate enough to have loving parents, grandparents, and great-grandparents surround them on a daily basis? From my experiences on *World's Strictest Parents* with troubled teens from broken homes, I know the answer: almost none. I treasure our time together on Sunday nights and hope Hatcher someday will come to understand how fortunate he is.

The farm in the late 1950's. Present day below.

Left to right: Sharon, son-in-law Chuck, Jennifer, myself, niece
Jessica, Brother Jim behind son Charles, Jorie (Jim's wife),
Lucy, nephew Mitchell.

Charles, myself, Sharon, Gabaga, Chuck, Jennifer and Hatcher.

Hatcher and me.

Chapter Twenty-three

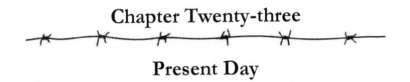

Present Day

Proverbs 22:6 says, "Train a child in the way he should go, and when he is old he will not turn from it." NKJV

Sharon and I have always tried to raise our kids, Charles and Jennifer, in the light of this verse. In our case, we have also had the added benefit of being able to raise them on a farm. Our kids have been totally immersed in life on a farm since the time they were young children, exposed to all the good things a farm has to offer. Some say, including my mother-in-law Gabaga, that Sharon and I worked our kids too hard on the farm. I don't agree. I believe that one of the reasons Jennifer and Charles turned out to be such outstanding adults is that they learned to work hard as children and continue to work hard as adults. They don't know any other way.

Sharon and I never forced our kids to work or do anything we would not do ourselves. During their very impressionable years, we did everything together, whether work or play, as a family unit. Jennifer and Charles saw how important faith, family, and farm are to Sharon and me, so these key elements of *Farm Strong* became important to them too. Both of them decided on lifelong careers on the farm to help preserve it, Jennifer as a veterinarian managing the family veterinary practice and Charles in the management of Hatcher Family Dairy.

I could not be prouder of my kids. Oftentimes, family businesses go out of business because of lack of interest from the children, but that's certainly not the case here.

Sharon deserves most of the credit for how well the kids turned out. She has always been the main disciplinarian in raising the kids. Sharon is also the glue that holds the family and the business together. She is the chief operating officer for the business and all things family, with just the right mixture of stubbornness and meanness tempered at the right times with enough compassion to handle even the most difficult situations. Without Sharon, there would be no Hatcher Family Dairy or *Farm Strong*. Although she did not come from a farm background, she is a true farm girl now and as much a Hatcher as I am.

**Jennifer with calf bottles;
she started feeding calves not long after this photo.**

Jennifer is much like me in many respects in that she has the same tastes for food and drink as I do, as well as the ability to handle major problems with certain calmness. The calmness characteristic is a trait passed down from my father. All her life, Jennifer has been wise beyond her years. She is one of the wisest people I know despite her age—just ask her husband Chuck.

Jennifer graduated from vet school at the University of Tennessee in 2005 with three major awards: the gentle doctor award and two awards in livestock medicine proficiency. After graduation, Jennifer chose to return to the farm to take over the vet practice so that I could work full time for the state of Tennessee as a staff veterinarian, becoming the state veterinarian in 2009. In 2013, Veterinary Practice News named Jennifer as one of the *Top 25 Veterinarians to Watch* in the United States.

My son Charles with his favorite tractor, *John Deere 4020*.

Charles, on the other hand, is more like Sharon and her dad Parker: set in his ways and not inclined to forgive easily, but under it all he has the same soft spot as Jim does down in there deep somewhere. Charles graduated in May of 2009 with a degree in Ag Business a few months after our creamery on the farm opened. At this crucial time when Hatcher Family Dairy needed to dramatically increase sales to meet our new debt obligations, Charles joined the family business and has become the face of Hatcher Family Dairy.

Charles is also instrumental in the management of the farming operation and the farm tours, as well as serving as the go-to person of local media for any dairy industry issues. The farm's gross farm income has skyrocketed since Charles began to apply his Ag business skills. Since Jim got married, Charles has taken the lead as the most eligible bachelor of agriculture in Tennessee.

Charles is also a poet, and I didn't know it. He is planning on building a log cabin in the woods off the southern slope of the big field, next to Jennifer and Chuck's house on the opposite side of the everlasting spring. Unbeknownst to me, in the solace of the proposed cabin location, Charles wrote a poem entitled the *Right Place*. His poem below and in the front of this book embodies what *Farm Strong* is and speaks for itself. I couldn't be prouder of the man Charles has become.

The Right Place

Every day there's a wonder of a normal life
with every bale that I cut with a knife
For I am the new keeper of this land
I feel like my grandfather is holding my hand
This very place is hallowed ground
With my last name I can be picked from a crowd
Nearly 200 years of family and farm
A normal life could do me some harm.

It can be quite mischievous from a stranger's eye
My ashes will be on this soil the day I die
Whenever there are troubles or doubt
I look up to the sky and know what I'm about
Just one glimpse of those pictures in time
I get the feeling of tradition and pride
What comes of this soil leaves a good taste
For that I know this is the right place.

Charles feeding calves.

Jennifer and Charles enjoy a very close sibling relationship. They would do anything for each other. Neither one of them is driven by money; in fact, that they have no idea how much money they have in their checking accounts. Hatcher Family Dairy would never have come into being if my kids, Sharon, and Jim had not shown the interest and support that they have.

Expansion and growth

From early 2013 to late 2016 Hatcher Family Dairy has grown from milking fifty-five cows to eighty cows in an attempt to meet demand for our milk. Despite our best efforts, we haven't been able to meet demand. Demand for Hatcher milk has exceeded our wildest expectations. Charles receives requests weekly from hopeful retailers that want to carry our milk products, but we have to say no. Without acquiring more land for our pasture-based dairy system, Hatcher Family Dairy has reached its ability to expand any further. There is no bordering land available around us, and we are being encroached by developments on three sides.

With expansion in mind, I had been looking for more pastureland in less expensive bordering counties for a few weeks with no luck when I stumbled upon a farm for sale just six miles down the road. The farm was named Battle Mountain Farm after a small skirmish that occurred on a hill on the southern end of the property between Confederate and Union troops during the Civil War.

Battle Mountain Farm is a beautiful 232 acre farm with over one hundred acres of pasture nestled in a cove surrounded by wooded hills on most of three sides with four small lakes/ponds. The farm could provide much-needed pasture for our heifer herd, allowing Hatcher Family Dairy to milk more cows on the home place and thus increase milk production. The farm was priced reasonably in our very high-priced land area only because it has some large power lines running through the property, making it undesirable for development.

Purchasing the farm was our best single chance of ever affordably expanding Hatcher Family Dairy in Williamson County. The involved Hatcher family—Jim, Sharon, Charles, Jennifer, son-in-law Chuck, and I—were all supportive of buying the farm. In my mind, the purchase of this farm was far less risky than the construction of the veterinary clinic on the farm in 1992, the decision to bottle our own milk in 2007, or the establishment of the creamery on the farm in 2009. Most people thought we were crazy to pursue these endeavors, but they all turned out okay.

The reality that I will be dead when the farm is paid off has entered my mind. I believe firmly that expansion is necessary as a way to secure the continuing operation of Hatcher Family Dairy for my children and their children—new grandson Hatcher Abram Yoest—and their children's children. We must take this leap of faith. My hope is not to sell or erode away the farm that has been in the family since 1831, but rather to grow it, just as my dad and granddad did during their lifetimes. Granddad added to the farm that his mother gave to him and dad added to what Granddad gave to him. I want to do the same thing.

When applying for a loan for Battle Mountain Farm with Farm Credit Services, we found out very quickly that the loan approval rested squarely on the good name of Hatcher Family Dairy as a business and the success that the family business had enjoyed so far. None of the Hatchers individually could buy even a portion of the farm, but collectively, as Hatcher Family Dairy, we might be able to buy the whole thing.

The loan application process put Hatcher Family Dairy under a microscope, requiring us to examine the business of the dairy very closely. A business plan had to be created showing how increased revenue could support the much larger debt load. Since the inception of the RockNRoll farm partnership between Jim and me in 1992, which currently operates as Hatcher Family Dairy, the partnership has struggled mightily financially. There were many years of running the farm in the red.

It was not until we added value to our milk by bottling it ourselves in 2007 that the farm began to slowly climb from a deep deficit. From 2009, when the Abe Hatcher creamery was built, until 2012, the gross farm income quadrupled. In 2013, the farm started making a little money. Since then, each month generally shows a little profit. Farm profitably is something that has been foreign to us until recently but is necessary for true sustainability. The increased farm income needed to support the mortgage of the new farm is based on increased milk production from buying more cows and also from the rental income from the three dwellings on the farm.

The three dwellings are a small, lodge-type house on the front of the property; a larger house elegantly nestled between two ponds at the center of the property; and a cute, rustic, small log house at the edge of the woods on the back of the property. A very large, steel-frame hay barn also rests near the edge of the woods on the back of the property for hay and equipment storage.

After weeks of deliberation, Farm Credit Services viewed the history of Hatcher Family Dairy favorably and approved the loan to purchase Battle Mountain Farm. Hatcher Family Dairy closed on the farm late in 2014. Although Farm Credit Services based the loan on increased milk sales, all of us saw great potential in also using the farm for events and agri-tourism. Farm weddings and other events held on farms are extremely popular right now, and the farm would help us capitalize on this demand.

Battle Mountain Farm is a great opportunity for Hatcher Family Dairy, but it is also a tremendous challenge. We began the long, expensive, and arduous process of gaining approval of what the county calls a rural retreat soon after closing the loan in 2014. If we could meet all the county requirements, Battle Mountain farm could be used for events in a farm setting. A surveyor, a soil scientist, and a civil engineer were all retained in preparation for applying as a rural retreat. One of the biggest obstacles was meeting the septic requirements for the amount of people attending the events to be held on the farm. We spent thirty thousand dollars before a stake was even driven in the ground in preparation for the planning commission meeting.

One issue after another seemed to be blocking any progress in the process, reminding me of the struggles at the beginnings of Hatcher Family Dairy. The massive septic system and an event barn needed to be constructed to meet the needs of our plan, not counting major fencing construction and remodeling of the cabin, the main house, the front house, and the large hay barn. Eighteen months and three hundred thousand dollars later, the county gave final approval of Battle Mountain Farm to be used for events, and a certificate of occupancy was issued for the new event barn.

A new exciting chapter for Hatcher Family Dairy has begun. If we don't go broke first, and our dreams for Battle Mountain Farm come true, at least one less farm in Williamson County will be taken out of farm production by development.

**The beautiful farmhouse in the center of
Battle Mountain Farm.**

There are seven Hatcher or Hatcher-influenced households on our farm. People ask us all the time, "How do you do it, so many of you living on the same farm?" The answer is, "It's not easy." We have the same problems most families do, maybe more. We are a functioning dysfunctional family.

At certain points in time, though, our family appears as perfect as a family in a Norman Rockwell painting—and then reality breaks in. We fight often and have issues with one another, as all families do. But if there is anything that our parents and the death and near-death experiences we have experienced together have taught us, it is this: we don't let the differences between us interfere with the love between us. Hatchers ordinarily speak their minds to a fault. The fighting between us ordinarily culminates quickly to a blow-up and is then forgotten.

After George's death-back-to-life experience, I began to

live a healthier life style than ever before. I have been watching what I eat more closely and exercising with Sharon, Jennifer, and son-in-law Chuck in hour-long exercise classes, circuit-training sessions, and boot camps four to five times a week. Except for my arthritic right knee and wrists, I am in the best shape of my life. The benefits of regular cardiovascular exercise are well documented. Exercise is good for the body, mind, and soul. It clears my mind and relieves stress too.

Originally, my basic components of being *Farm Strong* were based on faith, family, and farm. I've added a fourth component, fitness, because of its extreme importance in leading a happy, healthy life. If not for the boys at the YMCA—my wise counselors—*Farm Strong* may have never come into being, and they deserve all the credit for that.

In addition to regular cardiovascular exercise, I believe if a person is able, they should perform frequent hard physical labor all their life, as Granddad, Brimmage Tomlin, Douglas York, and Robert White did during theirs. Hard physical labor is missing from most of today's society, but I believe it is critical in keeping a person grounded, humble, and appreciative.

The journey to *Farm Strong* began the day that William Hatcher stepped off the boat as an immigrant in Jamestown, Virginia, in 1635. The obstacles and setbacks along the way have been many, and they continue today. Despite these setbacks, the farm has endured since 1831. The farm and those who live on it today are stronger because of the trials and tribulations endured by our forefathers and the continued trials and tribulations of present day.

Of the components of *Farm Strong*—faith, family, farm, and fitness—faith is the most important. If there is one thing my experiences have taught me, it's this: if faith in God is not put first, the strength derived from *Farm Strong* can't be obtained. The experiences we all have in our daily lives are not by accident but part of God's plan. My present-day life on the farm is a direct result of this plan. *Farm Strong* can best be defined as the strength obtained from and the shield of protection provided by an ever-present, almighty God.

The other components of *Farm Strong* are important, too. Family doesn't only mean immediate family but has a much broader sense. All people, as I learned from my nanny Lily Mae, are our brothers and sisters and should be treated that way regardless of type. Farm is not just the piece of land of which the Hatchers are custodians, but includes the knowledge and appreciation that food comes from Mother Nature/God. Fitness is being in as good a physical condition as you can be, along with the willingness and desire to perform physical labor if capable. Hard physical labor is good for the soul.

I once perceived people like those building the three-story sprawling houses across the road from the farm as a threat, but I now see them as potential Hatcher milk drinkers, possibly our greatest allies. Most people in today's world are three generations removed from any kind of farming activity and have no concept of where their food comes from or the hard work that went into it. We must educate today's world about the basic tenets of *Farm Strong*. These tenants are the same ones our country was founded on and are just as applicable today as they have been throughout our history.

If we can have unwavering faith in God, understand where our food comes from, have an appreciation for the work and sacrifice that has gone into the food, work hard ourselves, and see our fellow man as family, the world will be a better place. The future of Hatcher Family Dairy and the *Farm Strong* concept is in the hands of our consumers.

I am a tenth-generation American farmer. My son is an eleventh-generation American farmer, and my grandson will be a twelfth-generation American farmer. I believe in the importance of faith, family, farm, and fitness in everyday life. I want my children and their children's children to live and work on this farm as I and my forefathers have done. I have hope for the future. I am *Farm Strong*. I invite you to become *Farm Strong* with me, to spread the word, and to change the world. *Farm Strong* is the way to live.

To be continued.

Appreciate

Lumps of cream float bravely
on the coffee in my mug,
lumps of Hatcher dairy cream
a miracle of the modern day return
or rather that customary revolution
younger generations often take toward an epiphany
concerning healthy food, thinking they will be
the new saviors through health by whole wheat,
health by raw vegetables,
health by fresh eggs,
and health by cooking for oneself
the valued, special food their families devour,
for surely since centuries before the Mr. Graham
whose fame is anonymously kept
in the name "graham crackers,"
young parents again and again and again
seek to find the magic garden to plant themselves
or to find in trust in the farmers' markets
or at the very least to read labels in a supermarket,
and though one must admit that most don't.
Many do bake all the breads their families eat
and plant their gardens in defiance
of potato bugs, caterpillars, and the deer
(Oh that we were practical frontiersmen
who would kill the deer for venison
instead of loving them for the grace
with which they clear a fence;
and if we were, we could have gardens without
having to have barking dogs, but never mind)
and make their own yoghurt
so eagerly that in this generation

the brave Hatcher family starting its own
small farm pasteurizing and bottling operation
sells out its cream each week
before the next delivery,
for some personal family yoghurt makers
buy a full crate of the cream bottles,
depriving us ordinary mortals
of the joys of tender, pale yellow, sweet, smooth
food of angels, softer than babies' skin,
demanding of memories of grandmother's kitchens,
delightful, tempting Hatcher's cream.

So one might not believe that Hatcher's cream,
jewel of the organic,
home produced movement
here in Middle Tennessee
would be subject to difficulties,
dangers, droughts, water shortages,
the intrusions of modern progress
in the form of highways and subdivisions
but remember, oh lover of the precious,
that as the most beautiful of princesses might still face
the dangers of childbirth or a peasant revolt,
as the finest silver goblet can melt in a fire,
as the dearest high school senior
can die in a fiery drunken crash
after the graduation party,
just so can serious danger beset,
the loveliest cream,

the loveliest grandchild,
the loveliest mountain
which may fall to mountain top mining,
or the loveliest poem
which may never stay in memory,
or the loveliest star
which may fall into a black hole.

Oh, the dangers of the universe abound
so whatever the threat,
black hole or
water denying drought,
that which is loved,
which brings its own joy
that to which we run in body
or in the synopses of our minds
or perhaps only in dreams,
let us today
momentarily
seasonally
or forever,
take unto ourselves
in rejoicing.

S.R. Lee

Acknowledgements

Special thanks to S.R. Lee and Al Wild for editing the first edition of this book and for their support and encouragement while writing it. Also, special thanks to Kayla Fioravanti for her fresh ideas and help and coaching in the release of the second edition of this book. The family writings of my Aunt Martha, my mother Jacqueline Hatcher, my cousin Rachel O'Brien Melvin, and my cousin Bob Hatcher were used as resources in telling this story.

Many of the older photos from the 1950's and 1960's were captured by my Aunt Martha's husband, Reverend Paul Cargo. Thanks as well to Anna Christenson for her photography work and in the compilation of the family photos. I'm very thankful to all those who took the time to record this history.

Also, I want to express my appreciation to all Hatchers, neighbors, friends, and mentors for the impact they have had on my life and for teaching me the meaning of *Farm Strong*.

References

The Holy Bible, King James Version. Cambridge Edition: 1769; King James Bible Online, 2016. kingjamesbibleonline.org.

Hatcher, Charles. 2014. *The Right Place*. Used with Permission.

Hatcher, Reverend Jasper. 2016. *Hatcher Family*. Used with permission. Unpublished manuscript.

Lee, S.R. 2014. *Appreciate*. Used with permission.

Made in the USA
San Bernardino, CA
18 August 2019